1-800-GO

A LOVE STORY

Michael Farkas

Fear

He has not learned the lesson of life
who does not every day surmount a fear.

— Ralph Waldo Emerson

Love

There is no fear in love; but perfect love
casteth out fear: because fear hath torment.
He that feareth is not made perfect in love.

— 1 John 4:18

1-800-GOD-HELP ME

A LOVE STORY

Michael Farkas

Cover Art: Lisa Iris

ISBN 1-891824-08-2

Published by
Light Technology Publishing
P.O. Box 1526
Sedona, AZ 86339
1-800-450-0985

Printed by

MI⚡ION
PO⚡IBLE
COMMERCIAL
PRINTING

P.O. Box 1495
Sedona, AZ 86339

Acknowledgments

There is something very odd and wonderful taking place with this book. The book itself stands as a testament to the material contained within. Certainly, without the lessons that were shown to me in this text, I seriously doubt this book would have ever been finished. Truly, white-light magic and miracles do exist. Clearly, the principles of beauty and loving inspirational creation are at work here. When I can objectively detach myself from this process, I delight in how fortunately and synchronously so many wonderful things are presently happening for me. I am amazed at my good fortune and the joy of the friends and relationships that have developed as a result of this process.

It seems funny to me that I was able to come forth with the material in this manuscript in a few weeks. Strangely, it took only fifty-four years to get to that point. There have been such wonderful friends along the way.

I would like to thank Michael Mekjian, my very good friend and brother, for his strength, guidance and love for the decades that I have had the great pleasure of knowing him. I also want to thank his son, Dr. Michael Mekjian, for his help, guidance and friendship. The Mekjians are my family in every sense of the word. To Sue Hoover, for her gentle and kind heart. To Ed and Marilyn Hermann, for their council, friendship, love and for the continual support in all aspects of this book and their lessons of creative inspiration. To my very good friend and guide, Edward Breathitt III, sculptor and visionary, who for the past several years has always been there for me when life got very tough and who helped me to keep my perspective of the healing path of spiritual and emotional wholeness.

To my former partner, great beauty and teacher of physical hard work, direction, physical creation, intellect, strength of heart, physical body and loving parenthood; master of stamina and endurance.

To my angel, teacher, healer, warrior of truth of the ineffable realms of manifest and unmanifest light and knowledge, traveler of the eons. Her rainbow of colors is the love of all creation. Her contribution to me and others is beyond description.

To my wife, Laurna Farkas, who has been a great inspiration in my life. Her beauty and courage in the face of cancer and its cruel treatment has been the motivation for my life and for this book. Her contribution to me and others is beyond description.

Author's Note of Intention

When the material for this manuscript came to me, I was at a point of utter desperation. Every support system of physical, emotional and financial nature that I had built my life upon was in ruin and collapse. The material herein became my life line and guide at a time when nothing was left of my construct of reality and physical survival.

Initially, I was so thankful simply that I was able to connect with the knowledge and essence of the foregoing experience. I would have been quite content that the process stayed safely in my own journal as a record and guide to me. Also, I felt if anyone other than myself was ever to read it, it would hopefully be my son. At the time of its solidification to paper I did not know how much life was still left in my body. If I died in that period, at least my son would have some reference to who his father had been in life.

At some point, it occurred to me to share what I had been given with a few close and trusted friends. I wondered whether the lessons would be of value to others as it had been for myself.

I was truly shocked and moved by the various responses to the work. From that I was encouraged to pass it along to a less close group of friends and acquaintances for their reactions. Once again I was touched by the emotional and spiritual closeness that abounded in many of the readers. The majority of the readers felt the material was of a quality that moved them in such a way that it should be published for others to read.

The fact that it is being distributed worldwide is still somewhat unreal and unsettling to me. Because the nature of the work is about spiritual reintegration and healing, it necessitated total honesty and remembrance. Whether that was possible for me, I wasn't sure, but the attempt to be real was foremost if the reconciliation with self was to be a meaningful process.

Much of what has occurred in my life, as it has been for many others on this journey, has unfortunately been about abuse. Self-abuse, denial and abuse to others and nature as a whole has been part of the human drama of life. Not until there is a reconciliation and healing of these destructive elements can there be wholeness and the gift of creation. Therefore, nothing in this rendition of consequence has been left out. Initially, I was scared and ambivalent about the statements within this manuscript being made public. I realized to say or do anything less would create a shallow and incomplete process. To do anything less than what has been set forth would be worthless. To do less than what was done might as well not be done at all. Anything less would constitute the same nature of hiding and deceitful stories that created a fabricated face to the world, resulting in the trauma of incompleteness and dishonesty that had led me to the abyss of spiritual disintegration and physical ruin.

I faced a dilemma. The nature of this work is about love and reintegration; only honesty will heal. "The truth shall set you free" is a paradigm of the universe. However, if the material in its statements and revelations were to inflict more pain on others, then the entire point of the work would be lost and perverted in its very essence. I had to be very clear that the emotionally abusive behavior I had participated in for so much of my life was not being acted out again. I had to be clear that my intent for the creation of this work was about healing and not a new round of hurt or vengeance. No consideration of financial gain could be a part of this choice to publish or make public this material.

I consulted close friends, health-care professionals, doctors, psychologists and attorneys in an attempt to understand how this work might create anything but positive change and healing. At this point prior to press I am convinced that I am living my truth in this book. I am convinced that my intentions are real and honest and done in the name of love and compassion.

Several years ago, I worked on a film project that dealt with child abuse. Over and over again I interviewed and worked with people trapped in the nightmarish hell of physical and emotional abuse. Over and over again I worked with the victims of this human aberration and disease.

Early on the form of my research took on a particular pattern of discovery. Although it was difficult for most of the victims to speak about the abuse inflicted on them, they did so with one clear intention: to heal the wounds of this trauma they had experienced as babies, children and older individuals. Healing was their goal — for themselves and for others.

In almost every case the victims desired to mend the heartbreak of having been violated by someone who abused them instead of loved them. Often it was a father or an uncle or grandfather who abused an innocent's trust.

To many of the victims, emotional and sexual wounds, even decades later, still felt fresh, as if they had been inflicted yesterday, still open and unhealed. Some, if not the majority, had various coping mechanisms that allowed them to conduct their lives with various degrees of viability. However, the loss of trust and the pain inflicted on them often had profound influences on their health, self-esteem and well-being.

So often the victims wished that they could heal, speak with or at least find a channel through which they could confront those who abused them. In the few examples where this did occur, an amazing transformation took place. In that rare opportunity, the victim confronting the abuser came to understand that often the abuser had been a victim of abuse him/herself. Healing was possible.

In the vast majority of this form of abuse, that type of healing never takes place. If the abused gains an equilibrium emotionally, it is most often achieved by self-acceptance and counseling. Rarely does the abuser come forward, take the responsibility for the acts committed or give the victim an opportunity of encounter and healing.

Usually when an abuser is contacted or confronted, denial is the result. "I didn't do that," or "He/she is making that up to cause trouble," are often the reactions. Guilt, denial and the fear of public humiliation or criminal prosecution is so ever-present in the mind of the abuser that he/she is just not willing to admit to himself or others what had been perpetrated. In so doing, the abuser is forever locked into the hell of fear, guilt and anxiety of the acts committed. No healing is possible in this place of dishonesty. It is my hope and desire that as a result of this material others may be able to tell their own particular stories in the spirit of self-reconciliation, reintegration and healing.

The form of abuse that I was involved in for such a long period of my life has profoundly affected who I am. For the above reasons, I felt it absolutely necessary to include various statements and experiences in the forthcoming material. At this point I don't really know what the results of such statements will yield. My only hope is that healing will result. If other forms of justice result, then that is what has to ensue. Darkness is a far worse punishment than truth.

In the foregoing text every effort has been made to protect emotionally and publicly anyone concerned. Some names, characters and locations have been changed to protect privacy and feelings.

New Year's Day 1998

Book One:

The Thanksgiving Miracle

A True Account of Joyful Human Metamorphosis in the Aquarian Age

A Channeled Communication
between a Man
and His Angel

For My Son

To my boy, who I love very much. I hope from this you will gain a better understanding of who your father is.

I can't live your life for you, nor do I want to. I can't suffer or protect you from the inevitable pangs of the growth process and life mistakes you must endure and learn from, but I can offer these insights in a hope that they will help you grow up to be the strong and loving man I know you will become.

Contents

What is the nature of an angel
if not a messenger?

What is the nature of an angel
if not a friend?
If not a guide?
If not a teacher?

What is the nature of an angel
if not a heart so pure that she is a crystal
that shines as a rainbow even if it has not rained?

Pure white, Kether, God's mind of pure energy unmanifest.

Pure violet, third eye, realm of knowing and intuition.

Pure blue, a voice so gentle, words that sing
the songs of nature's poetry:
The crackle of lightning and evening showers;
The song of whales on their world voyages;
Bee's wings fanning their queen;
Deep sigh of pleasure unbounded.

Pure green, a heart so pure, love that has no conditions:
Power of life to heal any pain, any sorrow.
Such beauty and innocence, a glimpse of which is
shattering in magnificent tranquillity.
Supernova, star's birth, universe unfolded.
Rapture blending mind into infinity.
Power that holds all relationships in place and in
evolutionary chaos.

Tears of joy and loving kindness.

Pure yellow, hara, center, balance.
Center of ki, Shen.
Divine window of physical body and presence.
Power to be human; balance point between
heaven and Earth.
The breath of fire, heat of passion,
center of the universe within.

Pure red, center of creativity and sexual bliss.
Two beings intertwined in tantric union and creation.
Beings once known to each other forever joined on all
planes of manifestation and remembrance.

Pure orange, the Earth, the Moon, the Sun, the ground,
the foot place in all manifest and unmanifest creation.

What is an angel if not these things?
Strength of endurance, sent on a mission
to the no-man's-land of earthly drama.

What is an angel if not a warrior so fierce as to absorb a
direct sword strike and heal a mortal wound to the flesh
even as it is penetrating body.

What is an angel warrior if not so compassionate
that she protects
even those who would hurt her?

What is an angel if not a being wise in nature's geometry
and passionate as goddess Athena?

What is an angel if not a being called upon
and answering with her
vision and rainbow of colors illuminating any darkness
and in any location in all creation.

What is an angel if not the white-light presence
of God's love and glory?

O N E

The Ordinary World

February 19, 1997, 10:30 A.M.

On this morning I awoke after a restless night's sleep thinking about and anticipating the questions I had for Angel. I sat down at my computer and began to ask, and to listen.

Good morning, Angel. Are you available for discussion today?

es, I am.

Do you have anything that you want to offer first?

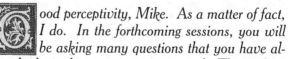ood perceptivity, Mike. As a matter of fact, I do. In the forthcoming sessions, you will be asking many questions that you have already devised in your conscious mind. That is fine, and I am more than happy to make the answers available to you. But at the onset, I would like to offer some ideas up front. Okay?

Yes, please go ahead.

know that you are quite nervous about this connection. I know you are seriously questioning your own sanity and wondering whether you should commit these sessions to paper. After all, who in their right mind talks to angels anyway? I know that you have very pressing financial decisions to make and hope that this dialogue will somehow benefit you financially. I have real concerns for your health in all these areas, but please let me ask you to approach this in a specific way devoid of such need and personal concern.

lease understand that your concerns are my concerns. I understand your pain and fear are very real issues for you. I feel your urgency with regard to solving these pressing dilemmas. I understand that all the questions you devised last night are your way of trying to cope with the difficulties you are facing. I know it all seems so complicated to get it right in this life. How does one get whole, you ask, when intuitively you know that all you are now is the result of an incredibly complex karma of past events. All these issues, all the complexities, how does one figure it all out?

o to address these issues I'm going to give you the answer to all of them in one word, and I'm going to do it now. You don't have to wait, or stay up all night trying to figure out all the right questions to ask me. This is a love story. That is what you are going to learn — all about love, just like you thought. Except, as we do this, you will no longer have to think about love so much as experience it. That's it. There's your entire answer. It is so simple, isn't it? Let me guess, you already knew what the answer was going to be the entire time, didn't you? "Well," you ask, "if I already knew the answer, how come I've been struggling with this for so many decades?"

That's exactly hitting the nail on the head, Angel. Let's proceed with the adventure.

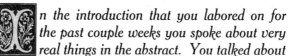

bviously, you have arrived at this juncture through hard work, trial and error and grievous personal experience. The fact that you are now here tells me a great deal about a very personal human journey. I know what is to be forthcoming in these sessions will be of benefit to others who will read this material. So please don't worry about anything right now. I just ask that you try and relax with all this.

In the following statement, Angel refers to the book that I had been struggling over for so long, and with little success.

n the introduction that you labored on for the past couple weeks you spoke about very real things in the abstract. You talked about suspension of belief and a leap of faith. Those are fine insights, but in fact you have been paying lip service to those concepts. I ask that you allow me to show you how to actually suspend judgment and take the leap of faith necessary in order to achieve the sustained levels of consciousness that you have sometimes experienced and to which you have often alluded.

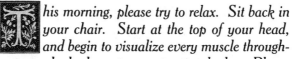

his morning, please try to relax. Sit back in your chair. Start at the top of your head, and begin to visualize every muscle throughout your body down to your toes, and relax. Please do that now.

In the next few minutes I did what Angel suggested in the way of muscle relaxation. On 12-12-96 the following poem was sent to me. Little did I realize at the time that the following poem, given to me months before this entry, was to be significant to the process I was about to begin.

Take yourself to a sacred spot.
Take yourself to a mountain overlooking a valley.
Take yourself to the sea.

Sun.
Moon.
Stars.
Planets.
All in plain view.
All at the same time.

Find a spot.
Don't be too comfortable.
Don't be uncomfortable.
Bring your totem.
Bring your sage.
Bring fire.

Ask sage's permission for cleansing smoke.
Ask Raven's permission.
Ask the Sun's permission.
Ask the Moon's permission.
Ask God's permission.

Ask for help.
"Oh, please help me."
Then wait.
And listen.

Still the mind.
Slow the breath.

Slow the heartbeat.
And listen.
And water.
And candle.
And fire.
And wait.
And listen.
Listen to the crows.
Listen to the ravens.
Listen to the wind rustle in the forest below.
Listen to the ocean pound.
Listen to the sand shift.
Listen to the bubbles and the tide.

Observe the motions:
The Earth turning.
The Moon turning;
The Sun turning;
The waves turning.

Listen to the wings of a bird flying by.
Listen to bees in flight.

Go within.
Listen to your heartbeat.
Feel the oxygen in your blood.
Feel the pulsation of blood passing through your muscles.
Still the mind. Say, "Oh, thank you."

Think of the red chakra, and the color red
as the color of your being.

the color of the Earth.
Empower that center.

Think of orange,
between your navel and the tip of your spine,
the color of creation and sexual healing.

A field of daffodils gently swaying in the wind:
The color of your hara;
The energy center below your navel;
Your center of humanity and justice.
Think of yellow, and know your humanity.

Open your eyes briefly, and see the forest of green below:
The pale green; the dark green; vermilion;
The green of the moss;
The green of lichen;
The green of the cactus;
The green of the pines;
The green of mistletoe;
The green of turquoise;
Think of this as your heart color.
Empower your heart.

Think of blue.
Think of the sky.
Think of the blue surf.
Think of the blue in turquoise.
Think of the energy center in your throat:
It is blue; it will give you voice
for all God's beauty that surrounds.

Think of the area in the approximate center of your head,
between and behind your eyes.
Pick your own color.
Think of magenta, violet, purple:
This is the color of the third-eye center;
This is the center of clairvoyance, telepathy
and knowing.
Empower that place.

Think of the area at the top of your skull,
and see it as the white light of the Sun.
Think of it as the white light of Christ's heart,
his soul and his love.
Think of it as Kether, the crown chakra.

Blend these colors.
Feel them.
See them.
Connect them to the world inward,
and the world outward.

Do not judge. Watch. Listen.
Do you hear it?
With eyes closed,
Raven's wings flapping, flying below.

t is fine that you did the exercise, but you did it quite perfunctorily as compared to how you normally do it. You are still very

*nervous and questioning this process. If you con-
tinue in this manner you will only get some part of
this session intellectually and lose the essence,
which really has nothing to do with the intellect. I
want you to start having fun with this. Get it? —
fun! The whole nature of the openings, as you call
them, is about pleasure. That's fun. It has been
such a long time since you have had any fun that I
would like you to start to think about this. Pretty
soon you will begin having it!*

*ou are always speaking about various hu-
man adventures in books and literature.
Obviously, the journey that Dante takes us
through is not a fun trip, although ultimately re-
warding. When Ulysses eventually makes his way
back home after years of great hardship and struggle, this romantic journey in epic proportions is not
only wonderfully entertaining, but speaks volumes
about myth and the human psyche.*

*hat journey might be fun for the reader, but
the hero's journey is never without its serious trials for the hero. In your journey, no
less an adventure than those previously mentioned,
you, Mike, can experience your long-asked-for adventure into the unknown. Do you get what I
mean? Think about it. You have been a
"blocked" writer for as long as you have suffered.
Right? Well, here you are writing, and there is a
very real possibility that somebody besides yourself
might even read this stuff and get something out of
it. Wouldn't that make you happy? See, you are
writing now. Don't you just love it? You are doing, right now, what you have always wanted to
do. So how come you are all tense and miserable
inside, Mikey? How come you are not really having fun with this stuff? What are you so uptight
about?*

ook, I'm not here to make you feel bad. I love you. I'm your angel. You asked for me to come and help you and I'm here. Let's just begin to address what it is that you are really facing. Okay? I will answer all your questions whenever you want, but the question-and-answer period feels like school again, and I know how much you loved that. In fact, can I take you back there for a minute and reexperience that little trauma?

ip-a-dee-doo-dah! We're here. I just love to say that. It's kinda like saying shazam! — which is another word I like. However, I know another angel who uses shazam! to get around with. So to not step on her wings, I'll just use zip-a-dee-doo-dah! instead.

ey, Mikey, you're still all wound up inside. My attempt at humor actually got a small chuckle out of you, but you are still a wreck. Take a ten-minute break. Go outside with Rex the king and enjoy the beautiful Sedona day. Take a deep breath and try to stop worrying about everything. Okay. Trust your angel. Right now, in this moment, you are fine.

I took kitty outside for a ten-minute break. Rex, a beautiful orange cat with long hair, immediately begins to roll over and over in the soft red clay in my yard. Once Rex begins to resemble an orange dust mop without a handle, he immediately goes into the house to lie on the freshly cleaned white bed sheets. I love that cat!

kay, we're back. How do you feel? Still a wreck, I see. That's okay, don't worry. It's all going to be fine.
Let's see, where were we? Oh yeah, school. We were about to look at the less-than-perfect experience that you had as a kid in school. First, let me

say, all human children born on Earth are blessed
with inherent joy and curiosity. I said all children
are born with this. Babies, from the moment of
birth, are in wonder and awe at the world into
which they have arrived. These little embodied
spirits come from the unmanifest universe by way of
desire and imagination of both themselves and their
parents. Being children of nature, they possess
within them all the stuff of the universe. Amazingly, each and every little being has within it the . . .

October 12, 1997, 4:01 P.M.

ell, Mike, where did you go? Let me see.
You cut me off midsentence about nine
months ago. I guess it has taken you this
long to ask for me back. What's the matter, Mike,
don't you believe in angels? — especially your own
angel, who loves you so much and has been trying
to help you for all these months and years. Don't
you remember when you asked God for help? Well,
I've been here for you ever since. You asked God,
on your knees, in your most humble heart, and He
responded. You listened for a while, got scared and
then stopped. I must say this is not an unusual
situation. People in desperation often do this very
thing. Temporarily, the terrible feelings inside them
subside, and they begin to believe they can figure it
out on their own. At this point, sadly, people have
turned away from their very essence, their very own
life force. I guess you would call it ego trying to
take control.

sually that lasts for some time, until they fall
again. The fall is worse in the next round of
fear and suffering. This can happen several
times until they either get so depressed that they
commit suicide in utter despair, or once more realize
that we are here to love and help them. I know the

*past nine months have been what you would de-
scribe as living hell. I have watched this and felt
this in you. I have cried and felt your pain and anguish. I have waited patiently for you to ask me to
return to your consciousness. The reality is, I have
never left your side. I love you so much and have
been assigned to you by God to take care of you —
for now and eternity. Can you feel my presence?*

Angel, I want so much to believe that you are really here.

*Mike, you have made some choices that you
are suffering with. Your suffering knows no
bounds. It is time for you to learn by your
mistakes, correct them and begin a new life. Your
mind has told you that this experience is called the
"opportunity" of crisis. That is a nice intellectual
term that you have cleverly thought of, but let's face
it, that term doesn't even begin to cover the hell you
are feeling every second of every day, which you
have ignored and in doing so have continued to be
out of sync with nature's laws of love and prosperity.*

As I hear you and write your transmission down, I do feel better.
But am I just going crazy? Am I just making this up so that I don't
have to think about my crumbling world out there beyond my
room and my computer? In the nine months since we spoke I
have fallen so far I can hardly endure it. I have no job and am
$40,000 in debt on my credit cards. The mortgage payment on the
house is going to be two months late in the next few days. My
wife, Laurna, has been in the hospital for the past three weeks
fighting cancer. I'm not sure I want to live anymore. I can't figure
anything out at all. My son, whom I love, is gone to me and his
mother will not speak to me either. I do nothing all day except
worry and try to get any job I can in order to save our home. I
can't believe my wife is fighting cancer and might not have a
home to return to from the hospital. How could things have gotten so bad? Compared to what I was concerned about nine
months ago, right now is like being in hell. It seems as if all my
worst fears are coming true.

would like to offer this to you now. You might or might not be going crazy right now. That is a human term that describes disorientation and madness. In some ways, you do fit that description. I know that it is easy for me to say, but try not to worry about that now. It is not important. I also know that you feel as though you are all by yourself and alone in your problems. I know that you are terribly worried about your wife, Laurna. You are sad because your ex-partner of seventeen years and your son, who does love you, will not speak to you and are afraid of you. You have been so hateful, scary and ugly. You have been so selfish and afraid. You must now accept this process if you are to survive this life and learn. You have tested death and your body and spirit will not allow your return "home" now. You are a messenger for others in this condition. Finally, you have dropped to the point where you have only Angel to turn to. Yes, this is a point of madness and total disorientation that you have arrived at. It is also a gift of perspective.

t is great and understandable that at this moment you are feeling better. You are feeling better because I am your life force and the light energizing your poor, beleaguered soul that has been suffering for so long. Please accept this transmission and continue to write the words as they come to you. Please do not stop. I ask that you do not question any of this. Please do not question or analyze any part of this communication. You have been chosen to hear this and to write it. Do not worry whether or not this makes you "nuts" or committable. In your present condition, you have few options to follow. You have such hurt and despair that most people will turn away from you. At this point no matter what you *attempt in the material world, it will not happen successfully. I realize this is a really tough thing for me to tell you, especially now, because you need it so badly. The fact is, your connection with spirit and creation is so shattered and dark at this point that you are barely alive. That is why you can't even get a job washing windows or being a waiter. Both of these are fine and worthwhile jobs of service, but with your energy right now, you probably couldn't do those jobs even if you were given a chance. You are in critical condition, emotionally and spiritually. You must learn your lessons now, or your physical health will soon go also. I am sorry to have to talk to you like this, but I am not telling you anything that you didn't already feel. Once you start to face what you have to deal with, you will begin your emotional and spiritual recovery.*

ight now, you have me. I promise that I will love, protect and guide you back to the light. You have embarked upon the most important journey of your life. I know that you can't understand this concept now, but your life situation, just as it is, is a gift that you are receiving.

Why do I want to turn away from you now? Why do I want to stop hearing you as I did nine months ago?

ou have avoided me for a long time. There have been so many offerings to you over the past ten years and beyond. You have asked, been given and then turned your back. You have been given everything you have asked for in the past. You have allowed yourself to accept some of the gifts, only to destroy all that has been given to you. So much love, beauty and prosperity has been yours. You wanted beautiful and loving women. You got them. You wanted prosperity. You got that and destroyed it. You wanted a son. You received the most precious child that God could bestow upon a man. You have, for the present time, lost that boy.

Of the greater levels of creations that you wanted, they were also yours, but those levels were predicated on the solidification of all the things you had asked for, received and pushed away. At this point you have God's love, Angel's love, but you are much of a pariah as far as most people are concerned. They "smell" your loss and dissipation. You do have good friends, but they are nervous and actually afraid of who you are right now.

I am sorry again to speak to you like this, but you know what I am saying is true. Michael, I am not judging you; I love you. Right now, once again, you are at a starting point for the journey and exploration you have in the past been afraid to take. Now you are standing in the doorway one more time. Will you go through the portal?

I could go on now and elaborate on your own particular difficulties, but that is not essential. At this point you know exactly how you feel, and all those who will read this material will have enough of an idea about your situation to be able to identify with your problems and your process if they are in a difficult life situation themselves. Once you begin to realize this material is not only about you, Mike, but the entire human condition, you will begin to get a valuable perspective on your journey and that of others in your situation. Pretty soon you will begin to understand that your life situation is a metaphor for the life situations of all those who read this story.

Angel, why do I want to stop this communication?

ichael, my sweetheart, you are so afraid of what you think and feel and are so worried about what others will think of you. Don't you realize at this point that you are here because you have nothing more to lose? At this point you are close to losing everything in the material world that you have — everything that you were given and everything that you worked for; everything you dreamed about and received. As for worrying about what people will think regarding your sanity, well, let's face it, most people already think you're nuts anyway. Mike, you take the wrong things too seriously. My sweetheart, I am not making fun of you, but you are a mess. You are so strung out at this point that you have been questioning whether you even want to live anymore. Of course, it will never come to that. Laurna was sent to you for that reason. You asked for her. She is giving you the lesson of your life right this very second. With cancer and pneumonia you see how your wife is fighting for every breath of life she has. Could you really take your own life now? You asked for and received your teacher. Previously, you were given guides and shown life and death. You sort of got it, but not really. Now you have no place to turn but to your Angel, who loves you and will carry you through this crisis and insanity.

Angel, I keep thinking about the outline and the *1-800-God-Help Me* story. I keep thinking about all the poems I received over the past year. What about that material? Should I start going back over that stuff now?

our mind is filled with messages we have been trying to send to you. As you begin to relax and trust, all that material will start to flow. In the past, you have been overly critical in your assessment of the material you were receiving.

You were so certain that the information was insignificant and boring that you consciously forced yourself to stop getting it. You have been at war with yourself for a very long time. You do understand free will, don't you? You have the power to make choices. You can choose to stay as you are or to recover your health and prosperity. I know you understand that intuitively.

You have a horrible self-image. You feel so guilty for all you have done and think you have done. Do you really think all those dreams you had about being a soldier and a killer in previous lives were just out of your imagination? We won't go into that right now, but you hate yourself for all those you think you have killed. Your memory of past lives' aggression is tangled up with your present earthly being. Even at this point in life when you are confronted with real-life aggressors, you are ambivalent about protecting yourself. You are so out of balance that you don't know who your friends are and who would hurt you. Mike, you are a mess. You are not unlike so many warriors of the distant and recent past who are in psychic-terror lockup. Why do you think all you care about is making healing films about Vietnam and about kids who are wounded and abused? Unfortunately, at this point you can't even get and hold a job as a window washer or waiter. You must heal yourself first before you can take part in the healing of others. The material that we are sending you will do that.

As you open spiritually, more and more material will come forth; just put it down. Let's take that first poem you were sent and share that now. Take your angel poem and put it at the top of this material. Make your next entry the thoughts Metatron sent you and make that the

introduction to the book you have been receiving:
1-800-God-Help Me. This is the book you have
been asking for and that I have been trying to com-
municate to you. Put it down now. Don't judge it.
Please don't judge it, Mike. See how easy it is?

know you are feeling better. I can feel it,
but please finally allow yourself to complete
this work. If you stop now, as you have in
the past, your anguish will build further. Believe
me, it can get even worse than it has been. The
book we have been trying to send you is your an-
swer and the answer that many of your fellow hu-
mans have been waiting for. I know you thought it
had a silly title when you first "thought" of it. Cute
idea, you thought. Once again you didn't allow
yourself to get the material because you belittled it
and thought it to be insignificant. Please, Mike, al-
low yourself to continue.

The following is the material I received several months ago. At
that time I knew I was headed in this difficult direction in my life.
At the time the following came to me, I was not in the spiritual
and financial crisis that I am now in, nor was Laurna sick with
cancer. At the time of this channeling, she was still working in
Tucson, but somewhere in my gut I felt it coming. The book was
the answer that came when in a scared and serious moment I
asked God in my most humble way to help me. The following is
what came to me before I stopped asking and returned to think-
ing that I could solve my life problems on my own.

1-800-God-Help Me

his is a little book of light, love, ecstasy and
creation for those who need God's direct
toll-free line for guidance and instruction on
how to make the transition from a life of crises,
filled with drama and difficulty, to one of constant
bliss and evolution. In other words, it's the how-
to-do-it book of joyful metamorphosis.

This guide will be extremely valuable to people who:

1. Are desperate and in serious trouble physically, financially or spiritually, and can't wait any longer for the right doctor, "big deal" opportunity or medicine man to show up.

2. Feel as though they don't have the stamina to last a second longer, is in a real emergency and is soon to expire.

3. Can't afford to be put on hold any longer, and must have a direct line to the Creator so that he/she can live wonderfully.

4. Want to learn the principles of wealth and well-being.

5. Don't find anything funny or happy anymore about their lives (the worst possible thing that can happen to a person).

In addition to the principles of love, beauty and creation that people will receive from reading this, they will be shown an overview of the remarkable human and planetary changes that are about to take place with the change in the coming new millennium.

The reader will explore and learn about the how-to of joyful metamorphosis. It is understood that many people on this planet are suffering with the accelerating pace of life and their disconnectedness from nature. It is God's intention that humans not suffer but share in the ecstasy of His bliss and light at all times. This guide will demonstrate how people can transmute their daily dramas and difficulties, no matter how severe it feels, and instead live in a constant state of God's bliss and harmony.

A Message from Archangel Metatron

*F*or those reading this who are not familiar with my name, I can best describe myself (in terms you might relate to) as God's chief spokesperson and archangel for the realm of the so-called unmanifest. Normally, in the course of human history, my position and accessibility have been extremely limited and available to only a few of the most conscious human students of God's universe. Inasmuch as I have no form and am part of the most ineffable aspect of all creation, I will do my best to travel the distance of distancelessness and speak the words of silence.

*A*ll reference to me and the nature of the phenomenon of which I am a part should be conceived on a level of symbolic interpretation. For example, the occultist of the West, the Kabbalist and the yogis and Zen practitioners of the East have developed various methods to trace our presence or to know that which is unknowable and speak of that which is unspeakable. So that the student can have something to draw upon, the ancient esoteric tradition of giving the student a symbol to meditate upon until it becomes born in the mind is used rather than an explicit instruction that would convey nothing to the student.

*O*ther human forms of expression have been developed in order to explore my realm. The tarot would refer to Kether, the first sephirah, as the Fool; its major arcana; and the four aces — Ace of Wands (force of fire), Ace of Cups (force of water), Ace of Swords (force of air) and Ace of Pentacles (powers of Earth) — as its minor arcana. The aforementioned all signify new beginnings and renewal. These symbolic references address the matrix of elemental states of formation and creation in

the physical realm of human manifestation and being. Cause and effect are not relevant considera-
tions so much as the yin-and-yang relationships expressed in Taoist traditions.

*T*herefore, for me to convey some aspect of the unknowable to the human mind, I set about directing
my message to the human subconscious in a word-
based set of symbols. For me to express an idea
about the nature from which I come, I would express this: Kether is the Malkuth of the unmanifest.
The limitless ocean of negative light does not proceed from a center, for it is centerless, but it concen-
trates a center, which is the number one of the
manifested sephiroth: Kether, the crown, the first sephirah. The description in your language means
nothing. Spoken in the previous terms, the listeners
schooled in English will be served only if they are
shattering conceptual notions about time and space.

*T*he reality of the phenomenon of which I speak
cannot be rendered in your language. Concepts of a
time-space continuum are meaningless when refer-
ring to the nondimensional realm of which I speak.
Throw away all concepts that occur to your mind
and begin to experience the following text mindlessly
and symbolically.

*O*ther parts of your beings are receptors of the
consciousness of the ages. The power being re-
ferred to is definite but undefinable in your vo-
cabulary of current speculation and theory with regard to "modern" physics. The nature of the
forthcoming message addresses the very basic principles of nature's creations, of which you are all a
part. To attempt to understand these forces would
be as futile as trying to put a gallon of liquid in a
one-quart container. These principles simply don't
fit into the human mind; however, they apply

absolutely to your beings. The energy that will be physically conveyed to the students of this material will most assuredly have a profound influence on those beings' health, intelligence and prosperity. The fact that it is not being taught as principles to be learned and digested, later to be acted upon, is fundamental to this process. Simply the awareness of these realms creates a magnetic change in those beings who are consciously connected with this energy field.

F or those of you who are truly suffering the pains of guilt, remorse and loss of the life-force spirit, know that ineffable help from the cosmos is always there for you. No matter how terrible your difficulty, whether you are so hurt that suicide seems to be your only answer, I assure you that all the loving and beautiful resources of nature are available to you. Renewal in this life is always yours for the asking. There really is nothing to learn or digest. One can speculate about these forces, but doubt in this regard most definitely tends to bend or dilute the flow of natural-resource energies attempting to penetrate the human individuals who second-guess or intellectualize the process.

T here is of course nothing good or bad about trying to understand the essence of the natural reservoir of energy. Intellect is a part of human consciousness that has been developing at an arithmetic rate in terms of human history and evolution of the physical human being. However, in the future, senses of extraordinary awareness that have absolutely nothing to do with intellect will become part of the human scheme. These still-infantile and mostly unformed organs, even in the most evolved humans on the Earth plane, will in 2300 Earth years begin to develop organizationally in terms of the biochemistry necessary to detect and cocreate spheres of physical manifestation not yet even conceived of in human speculation.

We understand that the pace of life on Earth has sped up to near-panic frenzy. The planet seems near nuclear destruction and humans feel more detached from nature than at any time in history. Human alienation is the worst it has been in all of humanity's time on Earth. We are aware of this. We feel your pain and recognize the need for help. Let me say, the beauty and ecstasy of life is close to all of you. Let it be known that the human race is on the verge of a remarkable shift in loving consciousness.

Many things are dying out on your planet. You are all feeling the birth pangs of a new era in human history. The labor is painful, but the birth of a new humanity is a magnificent evolution of humankind. Many of you are suffering, but the blissful pleasure of humanity as God intended is close at hand. A course of renewal is here within the pages of this book for those of you who are at a critical juncture in your lives.

Metatron

The essence of Metatron's message is about reinforcing your understanding of nature's framework. Please believe there are many elements and spheres of experience, manifest and unmanifest, in this universe. The nature of your being, Mike, is not to be taken for granted. That is why it is futile to try to understand and control your life from the perspective of perception.

Many, if not most, humans believe they are getting an accurate view of the world through their senses. They believe they can navigate through life pretty well on what they perceive. Actually, in the most mundane way, humans can go about their daily business pretty well using only the sensory awareness of the so-called basic senses. In actuality, the processes that brought you here and keep you alive are beyond your intellectual ability to understand.

oing about daily life is fine if left to the senses. Socialization and survival — that is, doing the basics of living, like feeding yourself, reproducing and interacting with others — can be handled quite well using common awareness on a conscious level. However, given the continual disharmony and conflict that is plaguing your race, it is obvious that running your lives using common awareness leaves a lot to be desired and is, in fact, a gross and inefficient way of perceiving the planet you inhabit. Even with regard to the nonconscious elements of your beings that tend to guide and regulate your actions and interactions, there is a primitive and unhappy vibration to that facet of your beings.

t is for that reason humans must be able to access higher realms of consciousness in order to create beauty in their lives and have spiritually guided "control" of their lives. To control one's life from the standpoint of common awareness and intellect will always fail any individual in times of major life change or change of integration with life and major changes in the planetary conditions.

or example, most people are able to handle their lives quite well when the balance of life's circumstances remains fairly constant and predictable. You might say the elements of routine that are associated with having a stable family, stable job or income and a society that changes with *small and unabrupt regularity can be handled fairly easily. However, when there is dramatic change, such as is the nature of what your planet is experiencing presently, the level of disruption in the human consciousness becomes extremely acute. Agitated and fraught with problems that have causes outside the human ability to understand, the mind becomes incapable of coping in rational ways of adjustment.*

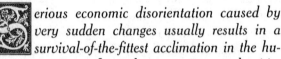 *erious economic disorientation caused by very sudden changes usually results in a survival-of-the-fittest acclimation in the human experience. In such cases, severe calamities bring on a disequilibrium in the social fabric, usually resulting in fear-based problem-solving and an aggressive use of the intellect to protect economic bases. Wars of mass destruction also ultimately result in this process. The twentieth century is an example of this phenomenon of fear, hatred and destruction.*

arfare of this magnitude has been called death in life. Even those survivors who have fought and killed in order to survive are left with an inner sense of loss for all those beings whom they used and destroyed by their aggressive survival tactics. In reality, all this drama of fear is totally unnecessary. The idea of scarcity that has been the foundation of economics as expressed in modern "theories of scarce resources" and is the basis of economy and allocation of those resources, has in essence placed man against man, family against family and humanity as a whole in a struggle with planetary resources. In fact, there is no scarcity on the universal level. In order to achieve sustained abundance planetarily, a readjustment of humanity's relationship to the forces of nature and those support systems that have created all things in the cosmos and are the sustainers of human endeavors must be established.

*I*f there is anything that can be said for the situation on planet Earth regarding the current struggle for survival and the nature of the chaos that exists very close to the surface of humanity's societies, it is the opportunity for a shift in planetary consciousness and human behavior. There are few people who don't either subtly feel or greatly feel the underlying current of imbalance. Even in relatively stable societies, crime, abuse and great imbalances in wealth are ever present. The prevailing feeling is one of humanity skating on thin ice.

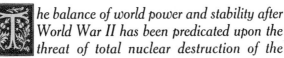

*T*he balance of world power and stability after World War II has been predicated upon the threat of total nuclear destruction of the planet as a way of keeping peace and preventing further warfare. How many times in the past five decades has the brinkmanship of geopolitics brought the world and all its creatures to the precipice of total destruction? Clearly there is a better way for the assent of humanity to its divine destiny than the road that has been traveled in recent times.

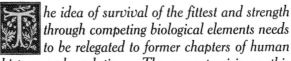

*T*he idea of survival of the fittest and strength through competing biological elements needs to be relegated to former chapters of human history and evolution. The current crisis on this planet that threatens to destroy all that has been created in manifest beauty and the essence of love can be, with human interaction, realigned to conform to the cosmic harmony of the Aquarian Age that is unfolding at present. Crises such as the current predicament in human circumstance as measured in population, earthly resources, pollution, disease and general instability can be the prime mover and

opportunity to bring forth a world of peace, har-
mony and the explosive creative potential inherent
in human manifestation.

Angel, I think you are losing me. How does this huge overview
relate to your being sent here to help?

ichael, my sweetheart, I asked you to please
write what you hear unabatedly, without
judging or trying to think about this infor-
mation only in terms of Mike. The difficulties that
you are personally experiencing, which I understand
and feel are very real and frightening issues for you,
are a metaphor for the world as an entirety. The
journey you are experiencing has not been caused
by your choices alone. You, of course, have made
decisions based upon a limited-consciousness belief
system that has, in part, brought you to this place of
near physical, emotional and spiritual death. You,
and all who read this journal, will learn to use your
freewill choice capabilities in the context of the
greater whole. What I am passing along at this
time is a small and brief overview of humanity's re-
lationship to its Creator. The present human condi-
tion as a whole is your condition personally. That
might seem like a very scary idea, but without giv-
ing all kinds of empirical evidence to back that up,
let me ask you to just accept that idea. Look at
yourself; you are scared and complain about the
precarious nature of your life as it feels now, but in
reality you still have food to eat, have your home
and live in a beautiful place. Your condition is pre-
carious and I understand that very well; however,
so is the condition of most all others in your world.
Some have more stable lives, more possessions, bet-
ter educations and better places to live than others
do.

he reality is, all of you are more or less in the same boat, going down the same river of life. The sooner you all get this, the better it will be for all of you. I laugh and cry at the horrible contest you have had with your ex-partner. You were both given so much. To witness the actions of the two of you is so sad and deplorable. Sometimes even you must realize how ludicrous the entire drama has been — the human comedy in its essential form.

oth of you asked for and were given a very sturdy boat to travel down the river of life's journey. When you destroyed your boat and found yourselves in the water together, both floating down the stream in the same direction, did you work together to at least try to find something that you and your family could float on? No. You both began fighting each other for the remains of the boat. You also engaged others to join your battle over the bits and pieces of what was left of your boat. Nobody seems to realize that you are all going down the same river, headed for the big waterfall that none of you will be able to handle. The waterfall is coming for all humankind. Choices can now be made to stop fighting with each other over the broken pieces of boat and instead learn to create a vehicle that will lift you all out of the current and send you off on a journey of love and prosperity to the stars. Sounds like a fairy tale?

ike, the journey you are about to take is the ineffable process of love and creation — an opportunity in crisis, as you have expressed it, a shaman's journey no less scary and exciting than any of the great epic poems or plays. Here you are. Here is the race of humans, too. You are all in the same boat going down the same river. You did not consciously ask for the current *circumstance of personal and global changes that have brought you here. You probably don't believe that you all asked for the play that you are acting out. So be it, you are all here and present. As Joseph Campbell would say, you have been called, and life's circumstances have forced you to enter the portal of your essence that exists in the other world. There is no turning back or place to go other than into each and every one of your individual caves of darkness.*

*U*nderstand, all of you, the path is scary and disorienting to the point of insanity. Most of the time you will have no clear understanding or idea where the journey is going to take you on the uncharted horizon of your being. But rest assured that angels, helpers, teachers and guides will appear when you need them.*

*A*ngel: The following "play" is Mike's. For all who read this material, your own personal journey will automatically fall into the places in the adventure where his name is mentioned. Do not try to figure this out, only read and meditate on the experiences of Mike as though they were your own.*

You are entering the abyss, the primeval void, the chaos before creation.

The following poems were sent to me on December 11 and 14, 1996.

December 11, 1996

There was a town.
It was a small and barren place.
Not many people lived there.

The desolate town was situated on the side of a
beautiful mountain, above a desert valley below.
At one time a vast, deep blue lake
flourished on the top of the mountain.

Before the drought,
a powerful river ran down from the
top of the mountain and through the lake,
to the town and to the valley below.

The town became the remains of
what had been a vast and abundant city of long ago.
The city had flourished with lakes and streams,
flowers of every variety, and gardens providing
abundant food and prosperity.

At some point, the people forgot about the power
of the river and its source
and they decided to place a dam behind the lake
to regulate the flow of water to the city from the
source at the top of the mountain.

And then it stopped raining, except occasionally.
And the tributaries that fed the lake dried up,
except for a trickle.

And the deep blue lake became a small shallow pond.
And the river to the city became a tiny stream.
And all of the city's vast population became so thirsty
that they all left the city except for one man.

The man held onto his home, but it was hard.
He carefully saved up water in small containers and
lovingly watered his meager little garden
and the few flowers that stubbornly refused to die.
Finally, there was no water at all.

It did not rain on the mountain and the tall trees
withered and died.
There was no water at all in the lake
and the few fish disappeared.
The meager little trickle
that had sent life to the town
was gone.
The man, in reverence to his Maker,
got down on his knees and prayed.
He prayed to his God in his most sincere heart
and said that he did not so much care about himself,
but he had great sorrow
for all of God's creatures that were
suffering and dying for lack of water.

The man's heart was full of grief and loss
for all the living things that he loved that were dying.
In his most sincere heart he prayed and asked God for help.
He asked God to protect all the small, helpless and beautiful
living things in the world that He had made.

The man began to cry.
At first there where few tears with his grief.
Then his tears turned to rain that fell onto the thirsty
plants and flowers in his withered garden;
the plants instantly bloomed.

Then it began to rain from the heavens.
Magnificent thunder and lightning signaled
the thirsty world below.
The dry tributaries grew instantly to carry
the bounty to the lake.
The lake became full in an instant. The fish returned and
the vast forest around the lake returned.

The dam began to crack under the tremendous
force of pressure from the lake.
At first, water trickled down from the cracks
to the town below.
As each droplet left the dam and reached the ground,
a flower would instantly bloom.

The man could hear from miles away the
sounds of shifting and pulverized concrete
breaking under pressure.
The sounds of rebar and steel stretching and
snapping echoed in the distance.
The man was afraid of the torrent that was going to be
released onto the town as the vast power
of the river was released from
the disintegrating dam.

The sound of the last crack of the dam as it finally
gave way to the pressure reverberated through the
man's entire being.

The man, in his garden on his knees,
hands folded in prayer, waited for the
tidal wave to reach the town.

The path of the water in its vast power,
unleashed from the broken dam, created
life, not destruction,
as it rushed down the mountain
toward the town.

The wave of water neared the town,
its size dwarfing the village.
The man opened his eyes and beheld the power and
the spectacle of the wall of water approaching.

As the swell came near,
the man closed his eyes
and thanked God for the life-saving force
that had come to rescue
the thirsty world.
As the huge wave began to fall on the man,
he sighed and took a deep breath.

The wave, of water took the man
down the river to the valley below.
As it raced, all in its path turned green
and flourished.

*The wave carrying the man
continued past the valley
to the ocean at the coast of the continent.
As the wave, with the man in it,
merged with the ocean, the water became the cosmos.*

*As the man moved at beyond light speed
through the galaxy, he became a star,
experiencing all of nature's love and intelligence.*

December 14, 1996

*Are you afraid to fly?
Are you afraid to soar?
Do you look at the birds with envy?*

*Stand at the cliff's edge.
Look back at life's circumstances
that have chased you to the edge
and to this place.*

*The only way is ahead—
forward, and straight down.
Look back at what has brought
you to the precipice.*

*Look forward,
only inches of ground
remain to the edge.*

Look downward to the bottom of the Grand Canyon.
Look down
and see the birds flying below,
looking up at the blue sky.
Look down:
the ground has run out below your feet.

The birds are here to help,
flying above, flying below, flying everywhere,
showing the way to freedom.

They call to you, "Jump! Jump!"
"Fear-stricken,
you tremble.

A nagging feeling in your stomach,
no way to go back.
Only forward, to
oblivion.
Such a beautiful day.
All is right everywhere.
So exciting.
So much hope.

So much desire to go forward,
to learn, to grow.
All you have to do is jump.

Ask for help.
An angel appears,
no wings this time.

Nobody else can see her but you.

Angel, standing there on the ledge
with you, looking down with a big smile on
her beautiful face.

"I'm here to give you a lesson," she says.
You look at her, love in your eyes.
Your heart is her heart.
Your breath is her breath.

She says:
"Watch me."
"Quiet."
"Get still."
"Pay attention and I will show you."

She looks you straight in the eyes.
A smile beams,
her hand holding your hand.
She says, "Now, watch."

She jumps off the edge to the chasm below.
Horrified, your heart drops
to the pit of your stomach.
A cold sweat begins to instantly pour off your body.

She calls to you telepathically. She is
far down now.
You see the specter of her fall.
She says, "Look, I'm falling, and I'm so scared.

I'm falling to my death."

She falls at a tremendous velocity downward.
She nears the ground.
At a certain speed, her wings appear
and open like a magnificent parachute.

Angel begins to fly.
The wind under her wings,
she ascends.

Angel hovers in the air
in front of where you are standing on the ledge.
You are still trembling.
She says, "Look, I'm flying.
Jump."

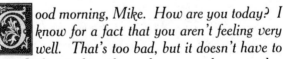

November 14, 1997

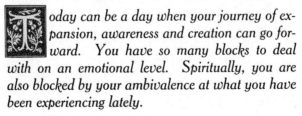

*ood morning, Mike. How are you today? I
know for a fact that you aren't feeling very
well. That's too bad, but it doesn't have to
last. In fact, today, if you choose, can be a wonderful day. If you choose.*

*oday can be a day when your journey of ex-
pansion, awareness and creation can go forward. You have so many blocks to deal
with on an emotional level. Spiritually, you are
also blocked by your ambivalence at what you have
been experiencing lately.*

hen I say, "I am your angel; you asked for me, and I am here to help and love you," you get scared about what is going on. In terms that you can relate to, you have been called for the adventure. You have asked many times for the knowledge and the experience. Every time you have asked, it has been offered to you! How fortunate can a guy be, anyway? Don't you get it? Every time you have asked in your most sincere and humble heart for something of great value, it has been yours for the doing.

he word "doing" is quite important here, for you in particular. If you desire to take a trip somewhere, that is part of action and creation. First, it is a desire, which is awareness and action. Your thoughts have put something physical into motion. Once you decide on your destination — say, you want to take a trip to Paris — you call your travel agent and purchase a ticket. Now, if for whatever reason you don't exercise your ticket, who do you have to blame for not seeing the pyramid at the Louvre Museum? You made the choice not to go. You had it within your power to go if you wanted, but you made the decision not to go. You also could have decided to go.

ou understand, you do have quite a bit of control over your life. Free will, as I have discussed, is an important part of the human condition and psyche. Free will is part of creation. The nature of creation is the entire reason why you are on this planet. There is so much joy in creating something. It is fundamental to a healthy human process. I feel the pain of all of you who are blocked in this area. It is so essential for humans to create, that it is no overstatement to say life without creation is a life devoid of essence. It is incredibly painful for any human not to be able to create. The *creative process is part of divine order.*

n the same way that God created the universe, humans create theirs. The process is nothing short of miraculous. Man, in God's image, creates his world in the same manner as God created His/Hers. The human process of creation goes as follows:

1. A person looks out into nature, God's nature and all of His/Her creation, and gets inspiration from the beauty and wonder of it all. At this level of inspiration there is no materiality. It is a feeling of joy and wonder — the divine presence.

2. From that place of inspiration comes an idea about something. At this stage there still is no materiality. Desires and thoughts are like waves of light. They possess no mass or weight.

3. At some magical level, as when a wave becomes a particle, a human idea takes on material form of physical creation. It might be a building, a painting, an action or anything devised in the mind and physically created. Whatever form it takes, it is part of creation from source and spirit. It is that part of life that makes all struggles worthwhile. In artistic form, it is a joy beyond explanation.

hen the process is blocked for whatever reasons, deep feelings of disconnection and depression will result. Not being able to create is the same as being cut off from your own divine source of life. Creative energy is the life-force energy unfolded.

Yes, Angel, I know that feeling very well. At times in my life I have had bursts of creative inspiration, idea and manifestation. It was so wonderful. Those experiences were truly the best times of my life. If I could only somehow recapture that ability. Just thinking about those times makes me feel great inside and optimistic about everything. I have so often wondered how and why the dreams came to me. The creative experience would happen, then for years it was gone. The misery and loss of that ability has been very difficult.

believe now we are getting somewhere in this process, my sweetheart. *Right now I can feel your life-force energy and happy feelings expand just from the discussion. The fact that you are hearing this and writing it down is so very important for you. This is part of your creative process.*

our process of creation is what we are here to discuss. It is part of the love story. God so loves His/Her children that He wants them to experience all the joy and happiness they can. She knows that creation was Her most joyous and wonderful experience. He/She wants all His children to be able to have the joy that He experiences in this way.

h, that makes you laugh, and tears are welling up in your eyes. Mike, that is okay. In fact, that is great. That is happy; that is where your life-force energy is. We are making progress now. Oh, joy!

ike, are you beginning to realize that you don't have to be miserable anymore? Are you beginning to realize that nobody has to be miserable anymore, that creative abundance is your inheritance and birthright as a human? It was God's intention for you all to have it — all of you. We understand that when you humans can't create, you literally go crazy, the kind of crazy that you have been experiencing for so long. I know it has been torture to your soul.

n the same way that it has been killing you bit by bit, it does that to humanity as a whole. When human societies are creative and productive, synergy on a planetary level happens. Life for all humankind becomes more than the sum of its parts. The European Renaissance is a good example of the creative explosion that took place after a thousand years of depression and disease. There have been many times of flourishing like the Renaissance on Earth in its brief history. This creative burst of energy of human potential is the unfolding of the divine plan for humanity. The age of Aquarius that humanity is now entering is a time like that of great beauty, love and creation on a planetary scale. I have mentioned that free will is an essential part of the human condition. Just as you have free choice to create the life you want, so does the human race as a whole. The divine plan is the hope of the Aquarian Age. It is, in part, humankind's destiny to either realize his great potential or completely destroy the entire race and civilization. It is your choice, Mike, to continue in your mess and pain, or have a life filled with love, abundance and creativity. In that same way, all humans have that choice. As an aggregate, humanity can choose providence or destruction.

s we have discussed, humanity has in the past taken various paths in its development that have led its current condition. Humans must build and create. It is an essential part of human health and evolution. Just as bees build hives and ants build hills, humans too must build and create. When humanity stops its divinely inspired essence of creation, it goes crazy and insane.

he destruction begins when people begin to feel lack in their lives. Simply stated, they begin to lose their ability to love and their *compassion and spirit connection. They begin to lose the joy and abundance that is part of the natural plan. They get scared and hostile. They begin to think there is not enough to go around for everybody. From that terrible feeling of fear, they get really ugly, hateful and envious of what others have. It doesn't take long in that environment to have humankind at total war with itself.*

t should be understood that sadness, destruction and misery is not a necessary part of the condition of humans on Earth. When was the last time that you heard God cry? Did you even think of that? Let me tell you, Mike, the saddest thing in the universe is to see God cry because Her children are destroying themselves, either individually or as a race.

Angel, I can tell you, for a long time much of what you have said has occurred to me personally. It all makes sense, but what do we do about it? How do we regain our love, compassion and creativity? How do we return to abundance from where we are now? How do I change my life and get out of the mess that I am in?

t is about time you asked me that. However, as I have stated, you have often asked (and in the correct way) and were given, only to ignore all the abundance that you asked for. This has been very sad for you. I know you understand what I am saying. It is not a question of your fault. Fault is not an issue here. The issue for you and for all humanity is getting it straight about how everything here in the universe works.

t is not necessary for you or anybody else to continue to suffer the vicissitudes of the ongoing painful human drama: the emotional high-ups and the way-down lows. The Aquarian Age can be the end of this type of agonizing human experience. We understand that what has been, has been. The nature of human development up until now has been a roller-coaster ride of feast and famine.

ike, how would you like to begin a new life? Right now, today. How would you like to be out of debt hell? How would you like to begin creating something worthwhile for yourself and for others? How would you like to keep your home, so when your wife gets out of the hospital she will have someplace to go? How would you like to start feeling good about life all the time and not just occasionally? How would you like to get beyond the negative drama that you have been experiencing for the past several years? How would you like to see your son and begin to have a healthy relationship with him?

Of course, Angel, it sounds like a dream come true. How do I do it?

ou must take a trip. You must get yourself whole, mentally and spiritually. You must begin to remember who you are and what you have experienced here in the universe. The journey and adventure that you must take is no different in principle from that which all humanity must take in order to regain God connection — that is, love, compassion and spirit. You must all remember who you are.

ot everybody is off the path on Earth. There are many individuals — millions, in fact — doing God's work of love and service. But for the rest of you who are really hurting inside and have lost your way, I invite you on a journey of transformation of spiritual and mental reorganization and reintegration.

ine months ago, when you were hurting and asked for help, we began to speak. But then you turned us off. Recently, you were really hurting again and you asked for help, and we started sending you 1-800-God-Help-Me. You listened for a while, doubted what you were getting and once again turned away. Over and over you have asked and turned away. Mike, it is your choice to do what you want in this area. But how much farther down do you need to drop before you begin to get it? Michael, I am your angel; I love you and can't bear to see you in so much pain. But it is your choice to change your own life. I will help you, but it is you who must listen, choose and take the first steps.

November 19, 1997

Hi Angel, are you there?

 es, Mike, I am here as always. Anytime you call me, I am here for you.

Angel, I am so scared. I feel as though I am slipping into an indescribable hell. Last night I watched the movie *Philadelphia*. The character of Andy became so real for me. I felt his destruction. I felt his life slipping away. I felt his pain and alienation of losing all that he was in life and the fear and hatred of him by the people who had been his friends and co-workers. At least he had a loving family that supported him in his journey. I feel so completely alone now. The family that I had for seventeen years, the only family that I have ever known in my entire life, is gone. I do have Laurna, but she needs me now to be strong and take care of her. I have lost so much in the past few years. I am struggling so hard just to survive. I am trying so hard to be a good husband and a good friend to Laurna in this time of her incredible ordeal with cancer.

 lease understand that the feelings of an unabated slide into complete helplessness are part of your process. You must understand this before you can get better.

Yesterday I went to the Ford dealer in town and applied for a job. At this point, Angel, I don't know if I am making sense or even relatable to anybody. I have been unproductive and feeling down for so long that I can't tell what I am saying to people. I really can't tell if I am creating anything but negative energy between myself and others. I tried to convey to the manager how much I needed to get the job and how motivated I was to do it well. Going into the interview, I was really hopeful about this prospect and the communication between the manager and myself seemed quite good. She knew that I had just that day come from Tucson after a very difficult weekend for Laurna at the hospital.

She gave me an application at the end of the interview and asked me to fill it out and bring it back later. When I left I was so elated. I called Laurna at the hospital and told her I had a successful interview and there was a real possibility of getting a job that could make a difference in our difficult situation. At five o'clock I returned with the application and gave it to the sales manager. This time she seemed distant and unapproachable. My heart sank. She said she would call me.

As I write this, I have no idea what is going on. The way in which the job interview at the agency came about seemed so correct; it happened so naturally. A few days earlier, I had lunch with the locksmith I had been working with for the past couple months. On that day I returned to him all the equipment that I had been using. I had hopes of getting a job here in Sedona that would give us some money to augment Laurna's income. After putting out $1,700 and several months of my time learning to be a locksmith, it became apparent the work just wasn't there.

Last Thursday, the day I had lunch with the locksmith, I accompanied him to the Ford dealer to open a car with the keys locked in it. While in the office, I said hello to the agency manager with whom I had an acquaintance but didn't know beyond greeting each other. I asked how business was and she said it was great. I asked if she was hiring any salesmen. She said that as a matter of fact, they needed another person to join the sales team. I was dressed in old blue jeans and looked kind of messy, but I ventured to pop the question anyway. I told her I would like the job and asked if I could apply. She said, "Call me at nine o'clock next

Monday morning." My spirits rose with the prospect of getting a job here in Sedona, a job that might be able to cover the mortgage and keep us out of bankruptcy.

As I said, Angel, I can't figure it out anymore — not that I ever could. Something that seemed so important and possible, like the job at Ford, started out perfectly and then went downhill. I'm so scared, Angel.

> *ike, you must understand that there are reasons for all that is going on with you now. You are on an important journey. This is your play, and you must live it out and see the results.*

Angel, you keep talking about a play and the journey. That is all fine and great, but right now it is difficult for me to get anything out of this situation but fear.

There are extremely few jobs here in Sedona for somebody like me. I tried being a waiter, and found that on the best days I barely made the kind of money I used to consider pocket change. Looking back, I wonder how I got to this place, where things are at near disaster materially, financially, mentally and physically for myself and my new wife of little more than a year. It might seem strange, Angel, but close to the surface of my awareness, I believe that I saw all this coming for as long as I have known Laurna.

I remember vividly two years ago this past July, the day that I first saw Laurna. She was at the car wash in Sedona, standing next to the Harley Davidson motorcycle that she had been a passenger on. The other riders were off their bikes and standing in a small group. Laurna seemed to tower over all of them. She was wearing black studded jeans and a black leather jacket with leather-fringed sleeves. She was wearing spiked high-heeled black leather boots that made her over six feet tall. Her long blond mane hung down to her mid-back. She looked so tall, beautiful and strong — a sweetheart, an angel in black leather. When I saw her there was a strange recognition.

About an hour later I was in my store sixteen miles away. I looked up and noticed that Laurna was standing right there in front of me.

I had an uneasy sense of destiny about this connection. There was something going on that was compelling, beyond the physical, a destiny I was afraid of, yet felt as though I could do nothing about. I saw Laurna a couple times over dinner and that was it for more than a year.

At the time I met Laurna, my partner of sixteen years and I were in difficult trouble in terms of our relationship. We were separated and both trying so hard to recover all the precious gifts that had been bestowed upon us. She and I had it all. I had asked God that I might have a family, a home and a business. All those wishes materialized so magically and so quickly. I can hardly believe what has happened. I wonder how it all came so easily, yet why is it so difficult to create anything now, Angel?

believe that you are beginning to ask the right questions now. I think that your process is beginning to show some light. You have begun your journey, Michael. It is a most challenging, but very worthwhile pilgrimage you are embarked upon. Your drama is about human suffering and human joy. You have at times harnessed God's magical tools of creation and beauty. You have at times forgotten all that you knew of the spirit and light plane. I feel how difficult it is for you to access your feelings and hear me speaking to you. You have resisted us for such a long time. Now your life is so difficult and so fearsome and fraught with problems that you are forced to turn to us because your realm of the senses and logic is continuing to fail you.

f you feel as though you are going insane, that is normal for the course that you have chosen. Many societies understand the nature of mystical or shamanistic evolution and consciousness. In your society people who are going through experiences such as yours are often drugged to keep them from going completely "crazy" from the journey.

ike, please try to concentrate on this and continue hearing and writing. You have been in total conflict with yourself for a very long time. Your connection is to a realm that few people ever see or witness. The realm is very foreign to most humans on Earth. Many people have a feeling that there is a spirit world, God or gods, demons or essences or angels, but most are deathly afraid of that unseen world.

ou have for a very long time been gifted with the power to contact us and to see our realm. I know that makes you feel very uneasy, and just writing this down assures you that you are on the verge of being committable. These concerns have come up a lot in our discussions here. You are at a point, however, where you are beginning to feel as though it doesn't matter about how anyone might judge you regarding this connection. You have tried to be normal for so long without understanding what that meant, and you have gone nuts trying to be something that you are not. You have been trying to be something that you have no idea about being, just as long as it is not who you are. This has been your unconscious desire. Your need to conform has resulted in the almost total closing down of your life force and ability to create. As we have discussed, creation is fundamental to the plan for humans. When people such as yourself stop creating, they stop living. It is a slow and painful suffocation.

our process now is to find out who you really are and regain your spirit and your life. You have been so afraid of this knowledge for such a long time that you are causing more and more psychosis in your system. The greater your pain, the more pressing your need will become to self-discover and find your source of light. Did you get that, Mike?

n normal everyday life, people go along and make their various adjustments. They pay their bills, make a prudent loan to satisfy debtors, adjust the home for the increase and decrease of their family size. They adjust their thinking socially and politically as the environment in which they live incrementally changes. Sometimes changes are an order of such great magnitude that small or simple course corrections do not have the scope for the adjustment. The size of the changes that are coming are so great that an individual mind cannot cope with the magnitude in terms of the knowledge or resources required to adjust. There is no technology available to construct economically a city that could withstand a Richter 10 earthquake. An entirely new paradigm is needed to address issues of such fundamental change. In order for an individual to adjust to the earthquake of a sudden huge shift of consciousness, which can be likened to an earthquake of major destruction to the senses, that person must go inside, and deeply.

n the case of shamanistic explorations and voyages, a deathlike experience similar to a major destructive earthquake shakes the psyche of an individual to his/her essence. All the pillars that upheld his sense of who he is are completely gone. In the catharsis, which can take days, weeks or years initially, a reorientation of various elements that constitute inner and outer awareness occurs. The ego is completely crushed in this process. It finally realizes it has limited ability and scope. Later, that part of the mind is reassimilated into a new context of integration with the normal world, as most humans experience it, and the other world, where the beings of the unmanifest reside. The shaman has the unique ability to travel the realms of creation and bend time and space in ways *other humans cannot.*

 nteresting, isn't it, Mike, that as you keep doing this it does get easier as it comes forth? As you begin to let go and accept what is pouring out of your being, you are getting more proficient in your ability to do this. I still can feel a lot of fear and resistance about what it is that you are reading on the screen. To have thought it was one thing; to be writing it down and possibly showing it to others is quite another. Correct?

Angel, before, I felt as though I had a great deal of time to produce something. I wasn't sure what that something was; I just felt it welling up inside me all the time. When I was comfortable, when money was no problem, I did not want to reach for the place that I now need to go. I had a family that gave me energy and companionship. With that companionship, I was allowed to go about my business of being stuck and suffocating.

Even as I write this material, which I am allowing, it is still very hard to accept what I am typing. I still feel that if *I* am putting it out, it must be bad, stupid and insignificant. Finally, things are at such a crisis that I feel as though every minute that I have left should not be wasted. I feel like I am dying. I wanted to die not that long ago to get over this misery. I was suffocating. I was disconnected from life. I was disconnected from the ability to produce anything. I was filled with rage, hate and fear. I wanted to love and be loved; but it was only an idea. I couldn't feel it. I was numb. I couldn't even connect with my own son. It seemed the harder I tried, the worse it got.

 hat happened when you got to that point, Mike? Who was your teacher?

First came you, Angel. I asked God for help, and a white-light presence would appear in front of me. Soon I learned to invite that beauty into my body. It would help, but I was still teetering on thoughts of loss, grief and personal destruction. Then one month and four days ago, completely without any warning that I would acknowledge, Laurna was given two weeks to live. She has become my teacher. She has caused me to experience and deal with my greatest fears.

 ow did you discover that she was ill?

Laurna was working in Tucson. She was so happy to have gotten her job, which she had worked so hard to get. She loved it. I remember the day the CEO of the company called to tell her he was making a place in the company for her. It was the day all our money had run out. We had just paid the mortgage payment with the last of her retirement account. We thought it was magical that not an hour after the money ran out, he called to tell her the news. She had worked for eight months for that news. We were so happy and relieved. We thought life was finally turning around for us.

Laurna has had a very difficult time of it for the past few years. To look at her and know her background, one would wonder how this could happen to someone so beautiful in spirit, body and accomplishments.

When she was fifteen years old, she had been accepted to Stanford University but chose to go to school in Arizona, where her family lived. She attended the University of Arizona, where she graduated summa cum laude in three and a half years. Her sorority sisters wanted her to run for homecoming queen because she was so beautiful and charming, but she declined because of her shy nature.

At twenty-six she became a vice president of an oil company in Texas. She lived the high life in the Texas oil-boom era that lasted until the mid-eighties. She worked for a man who started hauling crude with one truck in Abilene and wound up with a company that employed hundreds. She showed me her scrapbook with pictures of the company's Lear jets and her trips to Aspen.

When the oil boom busted in the eighties, Laurna went to work as a paralegal for a large law firm in Houston. In that capacity she worked eighty hours a week doing foreclosures and loan reorganizations. The law firm represented the largest banks in the state. She was called the "foreclosure queen" by her law firm associates. Evidently she did such a fine job that the firm wanted to send her to law school, which she chose not to do.

There are pictures on her desk that are reminders of her former life. One picture is with the former attorney general of Texas. The two other photographs show her at functions with the then-governor of Texas and with a former governor.

To look at Laurna, one sees a gentle beauty and physical strength. She told me what a rough city Houston became when everything started collapsing in the economy due to the deregulation of the price of oil. Bankruptcy, both personal and business, was common. She spoke about how so many families broke up during that horrible time. Everything in the entire economy was coming apart. Fear, meanness and hostility were everywhere.

One afternoon, in broad daylight, she was getting into her car after leaving a shopping center in a wealthy Houston suburb. A man, big in size, came up behind her and grabbed her from behind. He put his arms around her upper torso and clenched his hands together in front of her, locking her arms to her sides.

Without thinking, Laurna quickly turned around, even as her assailant had his arms clenched tightly around her. Instinctively and in an instant, she was facing her attacker, his arms still around her. Somehow she raised her arms up to his chest and grabbed his shoulders, pulling his body down hard as she raised her knee. In a second he was lying on the ground nearly unconscious. Nobody came to help, it all happened so fast. After that she got in her car and drove away, realizing the grim alternate scenario had the abduction taken place. A few weeks before, a girlfriend of hers had been abducted in a parking lot and her body was found in the desert a few days later.

When we got married, Laurna seemed outwardly so strong and powerful. She has a horse called Rush Taylor — Rush, off the racetrack. Laurna is a remarkable horsewoman. She is a perfect combination of gentle, loving spirit and firmness of conviction. It is always wonderful for me to see how she interacts with Rush. There is no question how much she loves that horse and who the boss is.

Laurna, who is forty-two years old and stands five feet ten and statuesque, had been a model for designers such as Valentino during her late teens and twenties. It pained me so much last weekend to see her in the hospital. So much of her beautiful long blond hair has fallen out from the chemotherapy. I remember her mother speaking about her hair as her crowning glory. Now the loss of her hair seems insignificant, given the fact that she is fighting for her life.

It is still inconceivable and difficult to believe that less than five weeks ago we went to the local clinic here in Sedona to see why she had been so tired for the previous few weeks. On that beautiful morning we went to the clinic three minutes from our home to get an antibiotic for what we felt might be bronchitis or, at worst, a relapse of walking pneumonia she'd been diagnosed with several months before.

When the doctor came to look at her, he quickly asked if he could do a blood test with results in ten minutes. I was alarmed. When he came back, he said her white count was 20 times as high as it should be and that her red-cell count was less than half that of normal. I asked him to step outside the room for a moment. I looked at him, astonished, and asked if he was telling us that Laurna had leukemia. He answered by saying that more tests were required, but that leukemia was entirely probable. He wanted to put her in the hospital right then and there. He was surprised that she was, in his words, "still walking around and not unconscious." He said in her condition she could have a stroke, hemorrhage or die at any time. She needed immediate hospitalization and blood transfusions.

I went back into the room where she was waiting and told her that the doctor wanted her to be admitted to the hospital immediately. I didn't tell her about the possibility of leukemia. She said she wasn't ready to go to the hospital, not that day anyway. We told the doctor we wanted to wait until later to check into the hospital in Cottonwood, fifteen miles away. He strongly advised us of the urgency at hand and the critical nature of her condition. Nonetheless, she wanted to go later that day or the following day.

We left the clinic and had a wonderful lunch with champagne at a local eatery in beautiful Sedona. That evening we got all dressed up and had another great meal with champagne at another fine restaurant in town. We were so close that night, both of us just wanting to be in the present moment in each other's arms, not thinking about what was coming.

The next day was fair day. The annual fall crafts fair was being held at the local high school, which was right across the street from the cancer clinic where Laurna had been examined the day before. She was very weak that day and I had to help her walk up and down the bleachers where the entrance was. I remembered that day a year before, just a few weeks after our marriage, when she had also been very weak and had to sit down often when we attended that same crafts fair. Whenever it would get hot, during the entire time I knew her, she would get very weak and needed to sit down. She always attributed her weakness to the aftermath of a heat stroke when she was in college. Somewhere in my being, I knew that something really wrong was in play. I knew when we got married we were both in for some very serious times.

We had been so individually weak when we got together. Laurna had not gotten over her beloved father's death from cancer two years earlier. I was still broken from the destruction of my former relationship, the loss of my business, the loss of my son and the serious legal battle that was ensuing over the breakup.

After the fair Laurna wanted to ride Rush. We went to the ranch where her horse is boarded on the outskirts of Sedona. Remarkably, at her insistence, she walked Rush to the arena, where she climbed on him by using the fence and proceeded to ride him bareback. Instinctively, the horse seemed to know that he should be gentle that day, a character quality not consistent with his normal personality. After about fifteen minutes on her beloved Rush, she walked him back to his stall. From there we went home, gathered together a few of Laurna's nightgowns and her toothbrush and proceeded to the hospital and the beginning of a dual nightmare: from Laurna's perspective, chemotherapy, and for me, facing the death of a loved one. Not since the death of my mother when I was nine had I ever had to face something like this. I never had dealt with the ordeal that my Mom went through; I didn't know how I was going to deal with this.

The ordeal commenced right from the beginning at the hospital in Cottonwood. The opinion of the doctors was that Laurna's condition was critical. Because of the overwhelming number of white cells in her system and the lack of red blood cells and platelets, Laurna was considered to be in such a precarious condition that her doctors gave her no more than two weeks to live if she was not treated immediately. After an incredibly painful procedure called a bone-marrow biopsy, which entailed forcing a ten-inch long needle into her buttocks and through her pelvis (while she was conscious and could very much feel the pain), her doctors in Cottonwood felt that she should be sent by ambulance to the cancer unit at the University Medical Center in Tucson. The biopsy verified the blood-cancer diagnosis.

The entire experience was happening so fast for both of us, as well as for Laurna's family, that we could hardly fathom what was going on. Upon arrival in Tucson in the middle of the night, Laurna was subjected to the first continuous and nonstop outer invasion of her body. The invasion of the cancer from within was already beginning to take its toll on her strength and senses. Last Thursday I spoke to her mother at the hospital. She told me in a most-concerned manner that Laurna had a very bad night and that I needed to be there as soon as possible. During the previous three weeks, ever since Laurna had been admitted for treatment, I'd been at the hospital as much as I could. The trip to Tucson is two hundred miles. It really isn't that far, but at this point, when everything had been falling apart in every direction, getting there wasn't always easy. Our two 1988 vehicles are in a very tired and worn-out condition. One of them needs tires badly, and I am driving around without any insurance because money is so scarce. I know that I have been playing Russian roulette for quite some time. Before this slide began over a year ago, I thought nothing like this could happen to me. Illness had not been part of my life since I was a child, when I witnessed my mother's death. Right now, with no medical insurance for me, I am so concerned about what could happen if I got sick. As I sit here writing and smoking my last cigarette, I wonder, What the hell am I doing smoking? It is a habit that I recently acquired.

I must be nuts, having spent the past month in a cancer ward seeing, amongst other things, the destruction caused by smoking, and here I am — smoking. The other day at the hospital, I went outside for a break. In a place designated as a smoking area, a man wrapped in blankets was sitting in a wheelchair. He appeared to be in his late sixties, but it was hard to tell because he was so obviously ill.

His face was gaunt from pain and disease. He looked as though he had not shaved for a few days and his scraggly beard was unkempt. His complexion was gray and sallow-looking.

When my eyes caught his, the man motioned for me to come over. He asked me if I worked at the hospital and I said that I didn't. When he asked me if I would do him a favor, I said sure. He asked what my name was and I told him. He then said, "Mike, could you please reach around to the back of my wheelchair and into the backpack, get the bottle of vodka and pour me a cup of it into my coffee mug? Please do it so that the hospital attendants don't see." I poured it for him and at the same time, he took a cigarette from a pack that was on his lap and lit it up. He offered one to me and I accepted.

He told me that he was a retired colonel who had been in the army most of his life. He told me that he had made it up the hard way, starting as an enlisted man. He had seen action in Korea and Vietnam. His specialty was military intelligence.

He coughed terribly between puffs on the cigarette, which made me uncomfortable. He would cough and gasp for air in the most difficult way. He had a tube running out of his nose to an oxygen tank strapped to the wheelchair.

He talked about having no money, but next Monday his check from the government would be in his account. He spoke of the cancer that was claiming his body, his pancreas in particular. The doctors had given him a few months to live and he said he would like to take one last trip to San Antonio before he died.

He'd had three wives in his lifetime and he'd buried all of them because of cancer. The last marriage lasted for twenty-seven years. He had tears in his eyes when discussing that one. He spoke about how his mother had told him the marriage wouldn't last a month and how surprised everybody was that it lasted for nearly three decades. She had died three years earlier. They had two sons, from whom he is now estranged.

He seems so completely alone and destitute and now at the end of his life. As two large military helicopters flew by, apparently coming from the nearby air force base, he discussed the many missions he had made in such vehicles in Korea and Vietnam. He discussed having been part of the team that developed an infantry weapon that could fire a small atomic bomb from the shoulder of one soldier.

November 20, 1997

ood morning, Mike. How are you? I love you.

Good morning, Angel. I had the best sleep I have had for months. I had the most wonderful dreams. I feel so rested and happy. The light came to me and stayed with me the entire time. There is a peace and sense of well-being that seems to be everywhere. I'm not scared about everything right now. I wonder if it will last. I have a feeling that good things are possible again. I feel so lucky that I've been able to write nonstop for these past few days. I have been able to do so without judgment and instead just let it happen. It feels as though some huge burden is lifting and I can breathe again.

ou are getting better. I am so happy that you are allowing yourself to be who you are. You are finally allowing your life energy to come forth out of the darkness. Your writing is your creative life-force vehicle now. It must feel wonderful after so many years of being stuck. It must feel like a good trip to the john after years of constipation.

Angel, I didn't know that angels talked like that.

o you remember when you first called on me? — well, actually, you called on God and He sent me to you. Anyway, I told you at the time, this is a love story and it is about fun. Do you remember that?

Yes, I do, Angel.

hat is the way it is supposed to be. When people begin making the change to love from fear, drama, hate, anger and need, they get happy. When people begin having the metamorphosis, they change. They get happy, creative and abundant. There is so much joy, fun and love to be had. So many pleasures abound in loving, fun, sex, food and the friendship of others. Laughing and joking is heard everywhere. In the condition of joyful metamorphosis, all good things become possible. Mike, you need to lighten up. I know that things are really tough now, but being dark and somber won't help anything one bit.

o you remember where you left off last night in our dialogue?

I do. I was talking about my experience of seeing Laurna last week.

hy don't you continue with it, okay?

Let's see. I had spoken to Laurna's mother on Thursday afternoon, and she said Laurna had a very bad night and it didn't look good. The doctors were also very concerned.

By last Thursday, Laurna had been undergoing treatment for three weeks. Her system was getting exhausted, especially after the doctors administered the chemotherapy. The chemotherapy drugs literally take a person near death, which was happening with Laurna. The drugs not only destroyed the cancer cells in her bloodstream, but they also killed off all her bone marrow and her entire immune system. While there is a good chance the therapy will kill off the cancer and put her into remission, it is a very dangerous time because she is very susceptible to infections and has no immune system to fight them off.

I awoke at two o'clock on Friday morning and got ready to drive the two hundred miles to Tucson. I was very anxious about what I would find. When I was there at the beginning of the week, everybody was worried about her condition. Laurna had developed pneumonia in the previous week. She had been running very high fevers and they were trying everything they could to treat her. At one point she had spiked to a temperature of 107 degrees. They packed her in ice and administered more antibiotics. Her lungs were filled with fluids and she could hardly breathe. The chemotherapy drugs were still in her system and no evidence that new healthy white or red blood cells had started producing, which she needed in order to fight off the pneumonia. Her blood pressure was critically low and the fever remained. The doctors were exhausting their arsenal of antibiotic possibilities. When I was leaving from that previous visit, her doctor said the next few days would tell if she was going to get better. She had been getting worse for an entire week and nothing was working.

With that in mind, I braced myself for the situation that I would encounter. I was really scared and didn't have any idea what to do.

When I arrived at seven o'clock Friday morning, I was heartsick at what I saw. For the previous weeks, remarkably, Laurna never really looked that bad. She still had her hair, her color seemed okay and she was lucid, but pain was ever present from the biopsies. Additionally, she was extremely uncomfortable from an infection that had developed in her esophagus. Because of this, she had trouble talking and could not eat. She hadn't eaten for a couple of weeks and was getting sustenance through a tube that had been implanted surgically in her chest at the beginning of her treatment in Tucson. She was on a constant supply of morphine for the relentless pain and she had a switch she could push for an extra dose of painkiller when the normal amount was inadequate.

On that Friday morning I was shocked at what I saw. The worst fears of the doctors seemed to be materializing. In the period of the previous few days in which they had hoped she would start to recover from the infection, she had not. In fact, she was getting worse. Her fever remained constant, her blood pressure was critically low and she was delirious and incoherent. She looked horrible. In addition, she could barely hear, which was a side effect of one of the many antibiotics being pumped into her system. Also, she had become extremely swollen from the treatment. Her legs and abdomen were filled with fluids that her system couldn't eliminate. Her legs were swollen to twice their normal size.

I spoke to her doctors, who were trying to decide if an attempt to drain her lungs would be worth the risk of her possibly bleeding to death from the procedure. Finally, they felt the risk wasn't worth what might be gained. They had one more antibiotic they had not tried and started to administer it to her early that morning.

Laurna's brother and sister-in-law were at the hospital. Her mother was at home in Phoenix for a couple of days for a much-needed rest. Her brother and I were not sure if we should get her mother back to the hospital, because her brother said their mother would never forgive herself if Laurna died and she was not there. He decided to wait until that afternoon to make that decision. At that point Laurna had not been taken to the intensive-care unit, and we felt, from that standpoint, that she was not in a place of imminent death, although somebody had called the hospital chaplain to her room. We asked the chaplain not to talk to her because we were afraid that she would get scared by the chaplain's presence.

By the afternoon, her brother had left to get something to eat and I was in the room alone with Laurna. At that point an amazing thing happened. Without trying to qualify this, especially given the context of this story, I witnessed a remarkable event. In Laurna's delirium, I heard a conversation taking place.

I felt the presence of three angels in Laurna's room. She seemed to be having a conversation with them. They told her that she had suffered enough and that she could come home now if she wanted. They were there to escort her if that was what she wanted. All she had to do was let go. Laurna, in words that were barely discernible, mumbled she had a husband that she loved, a horse that she missed and a job that she was anxious to resume. She told them she accepted God's will, whatever that was, but she had a desire to continue to live, get well and return to her life no matter how severe the treatment was on her body.

Witnessing this event brought tears of joy and inspiration to my eyes. I was deeply moved by her belief in God, her will and her great fighting strength. I recall once being told that "a champion is a person who gets up when he can't." That was Laurna.

Within the next few hours she made steady progress. Her fever abated, her blood pressure improved and she became coherent. By that evening all her vital signs had improved significantly. The fluid from her lungs began to decrease to the point where she could breathe with less difficulty. The doctors were hopeful, but they said that it still was too early to say that her condition was much improved or that she was out of danger. As I normally did, I stayed in her room that night. At about two o'clock in the morning she awoke from a very restless sleep, having an anxiety attack. It was the first one that I had witnessed, although her mother said there had been several in the previous days. Considering that only a few weeks before this she was "fine" and living her life, it was amazing to me that she wasn't constantly plagued with anger, fear and anxiety. I can recall only one time, for about ten minutes, when she first got the news of her illness in Sedona, when she cried for herself or said, "Why me?" Rarely in this travail had she ever complained, become mad or felt sorry for herself.

On this occasion, after weeks of treatment, huge quantities of drugs and antibiotics in her system as well as constant doses of morphine, she felt as though the circumstances were closing in on her. I called the nurse, who said she could give her something for the anxiety, but Laurna decided not to take any drugs for it. She simply wanted to sit up in bed, have her hand held and her back rubbed.

Because her breathing was so labored, even with the constant supply of oxygen, she was getting scared. As she got scared, her breathing became even more difficult. Although her condition was remarkably better than it had been twenty-four hours earlier, she was still capable of only the shallowest breaths.

It occurred to me to try and use guided meditation with her, hoping that it might calm her down. I would say, "Breathe in," and she would take in a painfully small and shallow breath. I would say, "Breathe out," and she would do her best to follow. Her lung capacity was still very diminished, and it was difficult for her to gain any sort of rhythm.

After a few minutes I augmented the exercise by saying, "Breathe in God's light and beauty; breathe out fear." We did this for a few minutes. Phrases such as "breathe in God's healing energy and health, and breathe out pain and illness" evolved in our exercise. It came to me to "ask" to find beauty — even in this situation.

Laurna calmed down enough to ebb the fear and lack-of-breath cycle. Our meditation worked to get her fear under control. After the meditation, which lasted about fifteen minutes, she was able to sleep again.

By Monday morning, Laurna was very much better. Her mother was back from Phoenix and I needed to go home and attempt to take care of our precarious financial situation. When I left the hospital, I was extremely inspired by Laurna's courage and the events that had unfolded.

The experience has caused me to make some very important shifts in my entire orientation to life. Whereas only a few weeks before, I questioned my difficulties even to the point of not wanting to live, I gleaned from this experience a remarkable understanding and feeling of how precious life is no matter how difficult things seem to be at the time. I realized that each breath is a God-given gift. Life is so precious that every breath is a miracle.

ow, you are getting it, Mike. I am so happy for you to have come to this place of gratitude. 1-800-God Help Me is starting to become real for you. You see that it is not just some "dumb little story" that you cooked up in order to make a buck to get you out of your financial dilemma. A few dollars or a few million dollars would have no effect on your real-life situation until you get the fundamental lessons about the miracle of life. Get it? You have in the past had lots of money and things, and the most important things you still didn't have. Mike, you are on the way to recovery. Aren't you happy to be writing about all this and feeling the power of it all?

I can't tell you how good it feels to just let go and express all the feelings that I have had all bottled up inside me for so long. Work is a gift. I haven't been able to work or create anything for such a long time. I can't tell you how good it feels to be able to write. I was always so afraid what I was writing was dumb and insignificant. At this point I don't care if anybody does or doesn't like it. I hope that somebody might get something out of this; but right now I just enjoy receiving this message, writing it down and learning the lessons of appreciation, abundance and joy.

 think now is the time for you to begin to look back and start to understand the many past experiences that have come your way that were consistent with your current realignment to the universe and your life spirit. It is time for you to learn more lessons about how to stop the ebb and flow of the fear-and-suffocation cycle. It is time for you to start remembering how to breathe and create beauty and providence once again.

I'm excited now, Angel. What do I do?

 want you to recall the first time in your recent history that you have made contact with the other side. I say "recent" because I know that you have been doing this for your entire life. You have always wondered, especially now, why things have gone so extremely well and easy for you at times, and then, as you like to say, sometimes a person can work his ass off, and the harder he works, the worse it gets.

 will tell you, when you have listened and allowed your connection to guide you, that things have gone remarkably well for you but because of your desire to beat yourself up and indulge your sense of unworthiness, you intentionally but unconsciously self-destruct. In this self-destruction, even when you ask and are given, you have not followed up with consistent effort and the dream and inspiration of creation leave you.

would say that given your current life situation, you now take nothing for granted. I believe that you understand how incredibly well you have done in the past. You have been truly creative when you have exercised your powers of spirit connection. When you think about the opportunities that you have created by asking and receiving, it must dawn on you what is going on. The current crisis that you are facing is difficult and very sad, especially for your wife; but in it, some very remarkable lessons are coming both your way and hers.

The most obvious one, and the most amazing, was my experience with Michael Sekeyumptewa, the Hopi man. In fact, I have as a reminder, right here on my desk in front of me, the beautiful piece of pottery he made.

Now that you mention it, I believe I still have the account of that experience on a floppy disk. When it happened about eight years ago, I wrote it down in script form. Let me see if I can find the floppy in my office . . .

Okay, I found it. Let's look at it. It has been a long time since I thought about that experience.

T W O

Crossing to the Other Side, Going through the Door

Exterior Day

It is a beautiful, cloudless day. The mountains surrounding Flagstaff, Arizona, are majestic in their beauty, rising high above the heavily traveled interstate. A late-model Ford Mustang zooms down the busy highway. Mike, a dark-haired man in his forties, is driving and Steven, eight years old, is seated next to him in the passenger seat.

Steven: Dad, we sure blew out of the house quickly this morning, didn't we?

Mike: We sure did. But you know, when I got the call from Michael to come up and witness the ceremonies, we had only two hours to travel the distance before it all starts happening. So we had to move fast — not a lot of time to make extensive plans. Let's call it an adventure.

Steven: What do you mean, adventure?

Mike: An adventure is when you are drawn to do something, and you just do it. It's something that you don't ordinarily do, so you can't really prepare for it. You don't know what the outcome is going to be or even where the experience is going to take you — you just do it. It's often exciting, unpredictable and sometimes even scary or dangerous.

Steven: Is this adventure going to be scary or dangerous, Dad?

Mike: Well, I don't know. One never knows these things in advance. You just have to trust that it will all come out okay. Sometimes a person is compelled to do something and he just does it because it is his nature. He doesn't consider the outcome. You know, son, I think we've missed the turnoff for the reservation. Let's pull off and get some directions at this fire station.

The Mustang pulls off the highway into the driveway of a fire station. Mike gets out and walks up to the roll-up door of the station. A big, friendly Labrador retriever runs up to him. He gives the dog a big hug. Four firemen are sitting in the station.

Mike: How's it goin', guys?

Fireman: It's been pretty slow this morning. But unfortunately, we'll probably get busy sometime today. We prefer it like this.

Mike: Maybe you guys can help me with some directions. I'm trying to get to the Hopi reservation, and I think I've missed the turnoff.

Fireman: Yes, you have. You need to go back out on the highway and head back in the direction you came for about four miles. You'll see a sign for Highway 130. Make that left and you are on your way.

Mike gets back into the car and heads down the gravel driveway, which is fifty yards from the highway.

Steven: So where are we, Dad?

Mike: We need to go back a few miles.

The Mustang pulls up to the edge of the busy highway to make the left turn onto it. Big trucks loaded with huge boulders race by one after another. Mike watches the traffic for an opportunity to pull out.

Mike: There sure is a lot of traffic for a Sunday. I wonder where all these trucks are going?

Mike waits for the next truck loaded with boulders to pass. The truck is approaching where the Mustang is waiting to pull out, about 100 yards down the highway.

Mike: Do you think we should pull out now? (Joking.)

Steven: Dad, I don't think that would be such a good idea.

Exterior Day — Long Shot

Mike waits for the truck to pass and pulls out onto the highway, and merges left, proceeding down the highway. Then the Mustang pulls into the left-hand lane and stops for traffic.

Interior Car Day

The intersection where the fireman told Mike to turn is marked with the Highway 130 sign. Big semi trucks zoom by in the opposite direction as Mike waits for them to pass so that he can turn left onto Highway 130.

Steven: This looks like the turnoff, Dad.

Mike: Let's try it.

Mike approaches the highway intersection, noticing through his driver's-side window that a small pickup truck is traveling along the street he wants to turn onto. The pickup reaches the corner and stops at the stop sign. The pickup is perpendicular to the Mustang waiting to turn left onto the street where the truck is stopped about forty feet away. Mike notices that the truck is driven by an elderly Indian woman and that there are two small children sitting next to her in the truck. Mike catches the eye of the old woman. He looks forward and sees a large Kenworth open dump truck loaded with huge boulders speeding toward him in the opposite left lane. The truck is moving sixty-five to seventy miles an hour and is about 200 yards away, pulling a trailer filled with boulders. Mike looks back at the pickup. His eyes meet the old woman's. She looks right at him and then her truck begins to move forward into the intersection.

Mike: Oh my God! She's going to pull in front of the truck!

The pickup proceeds into the intersection and begins a left turn that will take it directly in front of the Mustang. The big Kenworth continues at the same speed in the left lane as it approaches the intersection. It doesn't change lanes or slow down. Mike, with horror on his face braces for the destruction. Just as the pickup is a few feet from the left front corner of the Mustang, milliseconds from Mike's lane, the Kenworth broadsides the small truck.

The impact causes an explosion of parts coming off the smaller vehicle. The impact happens literally inches from the front end of the Mustang. Red engine fluids from the pickup spray all over the front of the Mustang as the engine block of the small truck disintegrates from the force. The impact does not even slow down the speeding Kenworth. The panicked trucker has left huge black skid marks on the road where he desperately tried to stop the rig before impacting the pickup.

The Kenworth, after hitting the pickup, continues to push it sideways down the highway. The small truck continues to disintegrate as it is pushed. The body of the old woman is thrown out as the door flies open. She lies motionless in the street in a twisted clump as the big truck and the remains of her vehicle continue down the highway until they come to a stop a few hundred feet away.

Interior Mustang Day

Mike: God! That was unbelievable. Are you okay, son?

Steven: Dad, that old woman, she's dead, isn't she?

Mike: I'm afraid so.

Steven: We were nearly in that, weren't we?

Mike: We are very lucky, son.

Exterior Day

The Mustang, miraculously unscathed, makes its left turn onto Highway 130. The emergency vehicles, from the station at which

Mike and Steven had stopped for directions, arrive at the crash site with sirens wailing. Emergency vehicles from other directions pass the Mustang, which is now parked on the side of the road.

Interior Mustang Day

Mike: How do you feel, son?

Steven: I've never seen anything like that before, Dad. I'm a little frightened.

Mike: Do you want to go home?

Steven: No, Dad, let's continue. I'll be okay.

Mike and Steven go to Second Mesa to witness Return of Kachinas.

Exterior Second Mesa Day

Seventy Hopi kachina dancers move rhythmically to the beat of their drums. They dance in an ancient enclosed courtyard that is surrounded by two-story adobe dwellings. The dancers are clad in animal skins and adorned with antlers and tortoise shells that dangle from their belts. They have headdresses of ornate masks or skinned animal heads that are worn over their faces. They move around in a large circle, slowly in unison. The group chants a powerful low-pitched hum that is eerie and takes on a not-of-this-world feeling. The onlookers, all Hopis except Mike and Steven, sit around the courtyard watching the ceremony.

The kachina dancers pass out beautiful baskets and dolls to the onlookers. A lady dancer ritualistically receives a gift of corn meal from one of the dancers. The kachinas dancers pass out gifts of food, as well as Hopi works of art, to the audience. Mike and Steven are among those who receive a food gift. A fierce-looking warrior kachina rhythmically beats his drum to the chant. The drum is beaten faster and louder until it abruptly stops. The dancers move faster and faster until they abruptly stop when the drum stops. The dancers file out of the courtyard. Michael, a tall, dark, heavy-set Hopi man in his fifties, comes out of the crowd of onlookers and moves to where Mike and Steven are sitting.

Michael: How are you, my friend? It is so good to see you and that you could come up with such short notice.

Mike: It is very good to see you as well. This is my son, Steven. I don't believe that you have met him before.

Michael: Hi, Steven. It is good to meet you. I hope that you are enjoying your visit here.

Steven: I am, very much. I wonder if you could tell me something about the dance we just saw?

Michael: Well, Steven, we Hopis believe that through the practice of these ceremonial dances, we are singing the song of creation given to us by Taiowa, the Creator. Time after time, we celebrate the deep mystery of creation, staging for the faithful an annual set of mystery plays underlying the creation plan so that it does not get lost in the shuffle of everyday living. We hope that we will be liberated through purification with the practice of these rituals; otherwise we may suffer to follow a path of pleasure, conven- ience, profit and personal gratification.

Mike: I'm sorry we were late, but we witnessed a very bad acci- dent on the way over here. It was terrible.

Michael: Was a small pickup truck involved in the accident?

Mike: Yes, an Indian woman and some small children.

Michael: That was my aunt Lucinda and her grandchildren in that truck.

Mike: I'm terribly sorry to hear that, Michael.

Michael: We just got the call from the Flagstaff police department a few minutes ago. You say you saw it happen?

Mike: We narrowly escaped being right in the middle of it. It's a miracle that we weren't involved. I'll tell you, I'm still shaking from it. The poor woman driving the truck never knew what hit her. How are the children?

Michael: One of the children died at the scene; the other is in critical condition at the hospital in Flagstaff. I wonder if you would mind telling my mother and her sisters about the accident?

Interior Adobe Apartment, Second Mesa Day

Four old Hopi women in their seventies sit together in a dimly lit, dingy kitchen area. They sit quietly, saying nothing; one sips liquid from a mug. Michael enters the room followed by Mike and Steven.

Michael: Mother, I would like you to meet my friends Mike and his son, Steven. I invited them to the dances today.

Mother: Hello.

Michael: These are my aunts Andrea and Corena.

Mike: I'm sorry to hear about your sister, ladies. It is a terrible thing that happened. But there is one thing that might make it easier to bear. I know that she never knew what hit her. It appeared that she never even looked to see what was coming. I saw her eyes and she just pulled out into traffic. It was horrifying. It happened so fast that she never knew.

Andrea: Did she suffer?

Mike: No, I'm sure that she didn't, it happened so fast.

Mother: She wasn't supposed to be driving. She had cataracts in both eyes. She couldn't see very well. But the children asked if she would take them to Flagstaff for the day. The poor children . . .

Mother starts to cry and Michael comforts her in his arms.

ike, can you elaborate on what you have just described?

As strange a story as you have just heard, it is really even more incredible than presented.

In reality, the story happened just as I presented it, except there are some parts that were left out, including what preceded it and all the events that followed.

I would guess it was about four months before Steven and I went to the reservation that Michael Sekeyumptewa came to my store. I remember that it was an unusually cool and windy day for that time of the year. In fact, because the wind was blowing down the street like a small hurricane, nobody was in town. The business district is only about two blocks long. The wind was howling and kicking up a mighty dust storm. It was no surprise that nobody wanted to walk around and shop in that windy weather.

I was in the store by myself when Michael came in. The three women who worked for us had taken the opportunity to get something to eat, because we felt the dust storm wouldn't last and people would be in the stores when it subsided.

When Michael walked in, it was obvious to me that he was Indian — in fact, a Hopi. I greeted him, as I did everybody who came into the store, and we began to talk. He was a big man with an extremely affable disposition. He told me that he had been a nurse in the Air Force and was stationed in the San Francisco Bay area. He had gotten, as he put it, a white man's college education, but he now lived on Second Mesa on the Hopi reservation. He said that he was a member of a medicine clan (I forget the name). Michael said that he had not been in my town before, but that he had come here to meet someone.

"I guess you are the one I'm supposed to meet," he said. I thought that was kind of an odd thing to say, but didn't question it. We chatted for about ten minutes before he asked me if I would like to come up to the social dances that would take place on the reservation in a few months. I told him that I was honored to be invited and would certainly try to make it. Then he left.

A few months went by and I had forgotten about the invitation.

The reservation is a couple hundred miles away and the Hopi social dances, although not a secret, aren't exactly a common topic in our community. And I must add that while Second Mesa is only a few hours away, it might as well be a million miles away in terms of a culture and a people. The Hopi mesas are the oldest continually inhabited communities in North America. When one leaves Flagstaff and finds the road to the mesa, it is definitely a journey into another time and place. The virtually straight, 100-mile-long, flat blacktop road is a trip into the past. When on it, you feel as though you are going back six hundred years.

The road travels a remarkably beautiful and totally uninhabited stretch of territory that belongs to the Navajo and Hopi Indian nations. In essence, driving the highway to these mesas is traveling in another country within the United States, a territory protected by treaty. The language, culture and customs are totally unique to the two nations. The Hopi reservation, relatively small in size, is surrounded by the vast Navajo reservation. When you finally arrive at the Hopi mesas, it feels as though you've truly gone back hundreds of years into the past. Except for a plentiful supply of Ford and Chevy trucks, the villages look and smell exactly as one might think they did in the fifteenth century.

I forget now exactly how it happened, but the morning that I talked to Michael was pretty interesting in terms of how it came about. Either I thought about the dances and called him to ask when they were going to take place, or he called me to attend. As it turned out, the day we went was the last dance ceremony of the entire season. If we had missed that one, we would not have been able to witness one until the following year.

The timing of that entire day was quite interesting. From the time Michael and I first spoke, Steven and I were involved in a synchronistic pattern: driving two hours to Flagstaff, witnessing the accident, continuing on to the reservation, where we would inform Michael's mother and aunt about the very important way in which Lucinda died, and participating in the ceremonies. I also had an odd feeling about Steven and me being the only non-Indians at the ceremonies. Recently, for whatever reasons (this has not always been the case), white people have not been allowed to attend the dances.

hat happened after that? Was that the end of it?

No, it wasn't. In fact, what happened at the reservation was only the beginning of it. The entire thing was so weird. I still have trouble with it. If this is a time of suspension of judgment and just allowing whatever comes out, then I will continue. As I said, the whole thing still gives me an uneasy feeling when I think about it.

It was about a month from the time that my son and I had attended the ceremonies on the Mesa that I called Michael to inquire about the child who survived the accident. After he gave me a progress report, he asked me how I was doing. I said to him that as a matter of fact, I had been having very strange dreams and nightmares ever since I witnessed the collision. He told me in a matter-of-fact way that his Aunt Lucinda's spirit was trapped inside me. I asked him what he meant. He said because I was looking directly into her eyes when she was struck by the truck and died, her spirit was trapped in my mind and was not free to go home to the spirit world. I would have thought the very idea of this was unbelievable if not for the images that I had been seeing and experiencing not only in my sleep but in my waking hours as well.

During that month I often felt as though I was somewhere else, and not of this world. I hadn't told anyone about this for obvious reasons. In reality, I felt as though I had died and gone to the spirit world.

The adventures there were quite amazing. I was among spirits and angels much of the time. In fact, Angel (and I'm really going off the deep end now), this phrase in the poem at the beginning of this story sparks a remembrance: "Pure red, center of creativity and sexual bliss. Two beings intertwined in tantric union and creation. Beings once known to each other, forever joined on all planes of manifestation and remembrance."

Reading this part of the poem has jarred my memory, and I am starting to remember how and where we met. Angel, it is so weird to have these feelings inside me now. I know I don't care what people will think about this (at least I have been trying to feel that way). However, an awful lot of things are coming to me now — wonderful things and things so far out of this world that I have a strange feeling about it in my stomach.

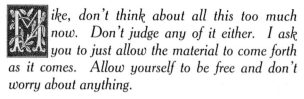

ike, don't think about all this too much now. Don't judge any of it either. I ask you to just allow the material to come forth as it comes. Allow yourself to be free and don't worry about anything.

Okay, so I am out there. What's new about that?

s there more?

Yes, Angel, there is more to tell. There are more parts to the story with Michael Sekeyumptewa and things beyond that as well.

Michael told me on the phone that I was *separated*, and so was his aunt. My body was still walking around on Earth, while my spirit had gone to the other world. His Aunt Lucinda's body was dead and her spirit was trapped in me. He attributed my visions and nonearthly experiences in the spirit world to the circumstances of the accident and my relationship with his aunt at the time of her death. Michael told me that I needed to set her free so that she could go on to the spirit world. He said that if I didn't allow this, the nightmares and visions would soon become worse and worse, to the point where I would go mad. Fortunately, Angel, you are requesting that I not judge any of this material, so I guess I can't just accept or judge that I have gone completely nuts.

on't worry about it, okay? This is your process and your integration. You are going though a spiritual awakening. I know it is difficult to understand, but as you understand and know intuitively, there is a great deal more to know about the universe and humanity's relationship to it than most people want to know. I grant you, it is scary at this point for you. You are also wondering if you should be writing this stuff down now. Let me tell you, there will be a huge number of people

*out there who will read this story and relate to your
experiences more than you can even imagine.
Please go on with your experience with the Hopis.*

At some point in the conversation, Michael told me how I could
free his aunt from my mind and allow her to go on. He also mentioned that because I had been on the other side, my understanding of the universe and experiences with it would never be the
same; that my life on Earth this time would be permanently different as a result of what I had experienced. Beyond telling me this,
he did not elaborate, as if he did not want me to know more than I
had to. He kept it brief and focused on the actual ceremony of
how to let her go.

*ike, I can feel your mind shutting down on
this right now. It feels like it did to me nine
months ago when we started to explore and
you couldn't face it and left. Don't you understand, if you continue to allow yourself to operate
on one cylinder (to use your expression), you will
continue to be shut down and suffocating in your
life? The entire reason why you are here now is because you are experiencing the crisis of Laurna's
cancer, which further exacerbates your very difficult
and precarious financial situation. You need to
open up. You need you stop suffocating. You need
to remember who you are and what you are. Stop
worrying about what others will think! I thought
we had already gone over that one.*

*ou are in a desperate living situation and
you need all your resources in order to fix
things. If you allow yourself to be stuck,
closed up and blocked, you could become a street
person. You need to wake up, open your heart,
your mind, your imagination and your creativity.
Just write this as you understand and remember it.
Don't worry about trying to sort it all out. Let others figure it out if they need to. Right now, just tell*

it like it is. Be honest and truthful, as you usually are.

on't have expectations about this — or anything else, for that matter. Have fun with this! Do you remember, I said that you are supposed to have some fun in life? Start allowing yourself to have it. Remember, this is a love story. This is a story about a guy who is going to become a hero to his sick wife in the hospital. You and I know right now that in Laurna's condition, there is nobody but you who can protect, nurture and love her. This is your chance to finally become the person that you always wanted to become. Because your angel in heaven, mentor and teacher has shown up by your request to guide your way, that in no way will detract from your mission on Earth, which means caring, loving and protecting your sick wife. As you know, I love you. I am your angel. You know the poem at the beginning of this story. I beg you not to shut down now just when you are beginning to open up. You don't want to be a street person, do you? Of course you don't. Do you know how really bad a situation that would be? Of course you do. So wake up! Think, write and learn.

So Michael told me to take my Mustang and go up Mingus Mountain to Potato Patch campground. He said I should take some sage and some food on a plate with me, and I did.

One early morning I drove six miles up the mountain to Potato Patch campground bringing the items that Michael had suggested. I parked my car in the rear of the campground and made sure nobody was around to see what I was doing. I took the plate of food, comprised of some bread, fruit and grains, and placed it in an offering inside the car. I took the sage bundle, lit it and smudged it all around the car, inside and out. Within a few minutes I felt Lucinda's presence leave my body. I felt as though I was back. From that time on for the next six years, I have been free of any surreal experiences like that, in my dreams, waking thoughts or actual experiences.

ou say you were free for the next six years? What happened then?

Sweat Lodge

The next six years was a time of personal and emotional stagnation for me. In the previous ten years I had realized a remarkable dream of inspiration, desire and creation.

In 1981, I was living in Los Angeles. I had been earning my living from the stock market since 1974. I had done pretty well as I think about it now, but not great. On March 27, 1980, a major market downturn ushered in a radically different life for me.

In those days I was living in Topanga Canyon, a wooded and rustic community adjacent to Malibu, California. I was renting a small house in the Fernwood district. I lived about ten minutes from the ocean. Daily, I would take my Labrador retriever, Gusto, in my beat-up 1967 Datsun "beach car" to the ocean and go surfing.

Gusto was a great dog and a wonderful friend. He was a rather strange Labrador, a breed thought of as water dogs, in that he was deathly afraid of the water. I would take my board and my dog to the water every morning and run up and down the beach a few miles to warm up and exercise Gusto and myself. Afterward I would paddle my board out a few hundred yards and surf if any waves were up. Gusto would run along the beach and bark with delight as I played in the water. Every once in a while I would pick up my ninety-pound dog and carry him out into the surf a few yards to see if he had remembered that he was supposed to be a water dog. The moment I dropped him into the surf, you would have thought I dropped him into boiling acid, the way he made a beeline for the sand. After a while I was content simply to have him running along the beach, barking with delight and watching me from afar. I'm sure it was also completely fine with Gusto.

On the morning of March 27, 1980, I turned on the TV to see how the market was doing. I remember the feeling I got when I realized I was caught in a panic sell-off. The news was that the Hunt brothers had caused this debacle in their effort to corner the silver market. In fact, the sell-off had been coming for weeks and I knew it.

At the time, my broker had assured me that it was a good time to be in the market. I was so impressed with the fact that he was a senior vice president of a large brokerage firm at an age decades younger than the other fellows in his position that I overruled my own intuition and took his advice.

I remember saying to him, a few days before I had committed my funds to buying a block of Amerada Hess stock on margin, that I was certain we needed to wait for the washout before getting in. He said, "Trust me, I know what I'm doing." "Okay," I said, "I will go with you on this, but I don't know why I'm doing it; it is definitely the wrong time. I should continue being in cash and out of the market here. I should be in Mexico with my girlfriend until after the bottom has been experienced."

Two days after I committed all my funds to this speculation, the slide happened. About two hours into the market day, I was in a position where I would be sold out the next day for being unable to meet a margin call.

At first I was horrified at being wiped out and broke at the age of thirty-eight. What would I do? Where would I go? After a while the whole thing became hysterically funny. After all, it wasn't my life. It was just money — stuff. So what? I always knew it could happen. After all, I was just gambling. I wasn't creating anything. I was just betting on the odds from my interpretation of the events that I witnessed.

About fifteen minutes before the end of the market day, an interesting thing happened. The market had gotten into such an oversold condition that there was a tremendous buying frenzy occurring. The final washout I thought was coming arrived and resolved itself by the time the end-of-the-day bell rang. My position was worth exactly what it had been worth when I bought it a few days earlier. I had been saved from a financial disaster.

After that really dreadful day, I began to question what I was doing with my life. I realized what really drew me to the stock market was the people in whose companies I would speculate. I so much admired the vision, hard work and success of the people who had the dream, intelligence and hard-work ethic to build something of value. I traded mostly in computer stocks in those days, and I loved to watch at a distance the plans and growth of companies like Intel and Advanced Micro Devices. I so admired the ability to create something from a dream. *I* wanted to do that. I wanted to build something for myself. I wanted a wife, a child and a business.

At one point, I was going nuts trying to figure out what to do or where to go. Actually, I had limited cash resources and not the best history of academic or business success. I was fine living in a pretty modest way, but I had no idea how I was going to get what I needed to attain my desire of a family and business.

November 22, 1997

 ike, you sort of dozed off. Where did you go last night?

I called Laurna at the hospital last night and we spoke for a while. She has gotten so much better. It feels like a miracle. She doesn't have a fever and hasn't had one for a week. Her infection seems to be gone, but the doctors are guarded about that. Her lungs are pretty clear and she can breathe. The terrible swelling that she had has decreased markedly and she can get up and walk around. Her hearing seems to be back to normal. Also, there is an indication that her body is starting to manufacture red and white blood cells; they are small in number, but it's a hopeful beginning. It feels as though she is on the mend and has passed the low-point crisis of a week ago. I don't believe she could have gotten much worse. I hope the worst is behind her. At this point, prior to another biopsy, there is no way of telling if the cancer is still in her system. We can only pray the treatment has put her into remission.

She has been trying to sleep, but anxiety is a constant problem for her. One of her doctors told her that she might be able to come home for Thanksgiving. I only hope she will have a home to come to. There was a note on my truck last night; I don't know who put it there. It said only, on a piece of scratch paper, the mortgage

number and the amount past due. It was odd in its informality —
just a handwritten note stuck on my windshield with only the
numbers. The mortgage company is in Florida. Who put it there?
Anyway, the payment is two months past due. I need to do something quick, maybe borrow more money from my credit cards if I
don't want to see a foreclosure. I so hope that the job at the Ford
agency will materialize. I went over yesterday and spoke with the
owner. He happened to be there and it was good that I had a
chance to talk with him.

When I went there, it was of my own choosing. The manager,
who said that she would call, hasn't. I thought at this point, I
might as well just push it to a conclusion. After all, it is a job sell-
ing cars. If I don't show them that I am willing to go after the job
aggressively, they might not think that I would be able to do the
job. I did see the manager who said by Monday we could talk.
Things are so precarious now. I realize that I can't figure out any
of this. All I can do is try to have a good attitude.

Last night I went to bed and the white-light presence was there. I
called for it to be with me. I prayed and asked God for help. I told
Him I was so appreciative for all I have now and that I accepted
His will. I had a wonderful sleep and woke up this morning full of
desire to write. I am so enjoying this burst of energy to write now.
Before this time, with the kind of life circumstance happening
now, I would have just been a zombie, able to do nothing. I am so
happy that this experience has allowed me to write my feelings
and give me some things to be happy about, in addition, of course,
to Laurna's remarkable recovery. I now know that the money will
come.

*ike, your healing process is getting stronger
every day. You and Laurna are traveling
such similar paths in this way. She was at
a low-ebb crisis last week physically, just as you
were emotionally. Both of you have turned the corner. Both of you have begun to tune into the universal love that is yours to access from your God
and your Source. This energy is healing your
mind, body and spirit. Your creative energy is*

*being released and you are beginning not to question
it and to actually enjoy it. Even though things are
probably the worst they have ever been for you
emotionally — with your wife's illness and your
unstable finances, certainly the most precarious and
insecure place you have ever known — still you are
getting* happy. *Isn't that amazing?*

I get what you are saying, Angel. In previous times I have intellec-
tualized this very thing, but even when I was financially secure
and everything was stable, I thought I could take care of everything myself. In that place I was still lonely, scared and closed
down. I would more or less ignore the insights that I would get.
The only time that I would listen was when things where dropped
on me like a rock, and I prayed and asked for help in moments of
serious difficulty.

ou *will learn soon to be able to access God's
love all the time. You will no longer have to
wait until you get into a life-and-death crisis
before you can tap into the love that we have for you.
You know that your angel loves you very much. I
am here to love and guide you whenever you want it.
You are beginning to remember that you and I go
back eons in time and have been together so many
times. Think about this Rumi poem:*

*Out beyond ideas of wrongdoing and right doing,
there is a field. I'll meet you there.
When the soul lies down in that grass,
the world is too full to talk about.
Ideas, language, even the phrase "each other"
doesn't make any sense.*

*ear Michael, your heart will lead you home,
in light and love. I have always loved you,
but you have forgotten how to love in this*

lifetime. You are beginning to feel that love now.

That is so beautiful, Angel. Thank you so much.

ou were talking last night about how you learned to achieve the desires that you had for creating a family and a business that you wanted. You were talking about how you so much admired that creative ability in others you observed. Can you continue with what happened?

It was truly a magical and wonderfully productive period of my life. Everything that I dreamed of happened in that time. It all happened so easily and naturally.

As I mentioned, I was at a point where I had a wake-up call about what I was doing. I was gambling and not creating anything. I was participating in a zero-sum game in the constancy of a created whole where there was only so much to go around — a situation in which some people came out winners and some people had to lose. That was the nature of scarcity in that game.

It was very much like Las Vegas — a fixed amount of cash being gambled between the players. Luck, intuition and the odds was the context in which the players traded back and forth the winnings and losings. Nothing was being created in that situation, just the ebb and flow of a fixed sum. In that environment there had to be winners and losers. Greed and fear, surplus and scarcity were the names of that game. That was the stock market gambling experience. The greed and fear resulted in emotional highs and lows for the players. Serious uncertainty always plagued the playing field. The feelings of competitiveness created distrust, jealousy and often hatred among the participants. The entire experience taxed the human physical and emotional system to the max. Even in winning there was the constant feeling that it could not last and the tide could turn the other way at any time. It definitely was not a place of love, respect or mutual creation.

Several years ago I was in Denver, Colorado. The downtown area was going through an economic revitalization. I enjoyed seeing the Edison building, a neoclassical, beautiful old building that had been there for many decades. It contrasted with the many new high-rise modern structures being constructed next to it.

It amazed me to think about the incredible growth period at the turn of this century, when really wonderful and positive dreams, ideas and human progress were achieved. Thomas Edison and visionaries like him around the world were making inroads in technological innovation that had started late in the previous century with the discovery of the electromagnetic spectrum.

This field of light has always been here in the universe. Only recently in human history has it been explored scientifically. Without focusing on how the beauty of that exploration has been perverted into the development of destructive technologies, one can only be amazed at how many great advances have come out of that knowledge.

Edison, a man of deep thought and vision, went "inside," observed God's universe and received inspiration from all that he saw. From those observations, ideas emerged that revolutionized the world.

Many of those ideas resulted in a synergy of human energy and teamwork that built a company based on the principle of natural law and is still contributing and growing in terms of economy and human well-being. All of us as humans need to build and create. It is such a joy to discover something and work with others to build a thing of lasting beauty and productivity. I so much wanted, in my own small way, to do that.

I had been so caught up in my daily gambling experience that I was lost from my love and creativity. I was drowning in fear and competition. I was just trying to survive. When I nearly lost all my material possessions, I was forced to once again go inside and ask for help.

One day not long after the wake-up call, I was sitting at my desk in Topanga and meditating in a deep and silent way. In that place I had no desires or expectations. I was simply in a place of quiet observation. In that place I had thanked the universe for all I had and was enjoying the peace I was receiving.

I had a dream. In it I saw a beautiful woman who was my wife. I saw a darling baby who was my son and a building that I was building with others. It was so clear and so real.

I awoke and looked on my bookshelf. In the collection was a book for high school students that listed alternative educational environments outside the normal university experience. One of those places was Arcosanti in northern Arizona. It was a community that had been started by the visionary thinker and architect Paolo Soleri. Soleri had been a student of Frank Lloyd Wright at Taliesin West in Scottsdale, Arizona. Soleri was building a community based on the philosophy of Pierre Teilhard de Chardin, the late French teacher and philosopher. Soleri was creating his town architecturally and spiritually based on the philosophy that Teilhard de Chardin theorized. The premise was the spiritual and social integration of humankind and the universe of love and divine order.

Other possibilities were communities that were being developed in similar ways in Scotland and Holland. Arcosanti was the obvious choice to explore because it was only a day's drive from where I lived in California.

Upon arriving there I found a wonderfully different experience from where I had been living and what I had been doing. Most of the people there were considerably younger than I was. Most were young architects and writers taking a six-week workshop to experience the philosophy and actually have a hands-on opportunity to build the town. In the mornings we would dig sewers and gas lines, tie rebar and pour concrete. During periods of the day there were talks about art, music and architecture given by Soleri and other writers and thinkers. While I was there, concerts were often performed by various members of the staff and students. We all ate together and lived together. The food was enjoyable and the provocative young men and women who attended the workshop were wonderful.

There were various levels of accommodations to be experienced at Arcosanti. The permanent members had their own apartments. They were small and modest, but had running water and bathrooms along with other normal amenities. We, the workshop people, lived in small wooden shelters called yurts. There were also tent accommodations down by the river. I shared a tent with a young architect who normally went to school in Boston, but was in Arizona for the summer workshop. Although crude, the structures we lived in were surrounded by the most beautiful landscape that comprised several hundred acres of pristine northern Arizona real estate. The experience was great fun, and I had my first opportunity to dream about a concept and actually participate building it with my own two hands.

After I had been at Arcosanti for a few weeks, some of the guys asked me if I wanted to go to Prescott for the day. I had not heard of the place before and they told me it was a community up in the mountains about an hour from Arcosanti. I thought it sounded like fun.

We entered Prescott from the west, passing through national forest at an elevation of 5000 feet. As we ascended into the town, there was an instant recognition about the place that made me love it.

The five of us hadn't been in town for more than ten minutes when I first saw my future partner. She was in her 400-square-foot pottery store making pottery on a wheel. I looked at her and she looked at me. She was a beautiful woman in her late thirties who had a mane of long brown hair and blue eyes. She looked nowhere near her age, although now, at age fifty-three, to me thirty-eight seems like a kid. We exchanged a few words and I left her store. I walked down the street into another gallery, where I met another woman. The lady turned out to be a good friend of my future partner. She told me that she wanted me to meet her girlfriend in a few minutes. At the time I didn't realize that I had already met her.

Within half an hour my future mate and partner and I were having an after-work drink at the local bar at the other end of the block. I don't think it was ten minutes into our relationship when I told her that I knew she was the mother of my son. She looked at me with surprise and cautiously nodded yes.

That was the beginning of a wonderful love affair and all the things that I had dreamt about. Within a few months she was pregnant with our son. She delivered our boy in our bed at home. I remember that he smiled at me within the first hour of his life. I was so proud. She had given birth to the most wonderful child. Two days after his birth I put him on the waiting list at the local Montessori school. I didn't want to waste any time participating in my son's education. We were so lucky.

My partner had a beautiful two-story Victorian house that she had restored. She paid for it by making pottery. Truly, she was and still is an amazing worker. She would work from sunup to late at night and never appeared to need a rest. Two days after she had our baby, I remember her going up the stairs on all fours because she couldn't wait to get back to work. She carried the child in a basket, which she took to work with her just a few days after his birth.

Over the next ten years we did a lot of building. For $20,000 we acquired a broken-down one-story building located a few doors from where her pottery shop had been, remodeling it into a three-story gallery that housed our store and gallery. It was the most gratifying and productive period of my life. I was so lucky, but I didn't really get it. At some point, instead of appreciating all that I had, I began to want more. I forgot to keep thanking God for all that we had. The dream that I had in Los Angeles had been granted and I lost sight of it all. I forgot the magical process of love and natural attraction that created all the providence and instead became attached to all the stuff. Within a couple of years after the completion of our building, the relationship was in serious trouble. The love that created all that we had was fading. We tried for several painful years to get it right, but it wasn't happening.

By the winter of 1994 we were so estranged that neither of us knew how to recover the essence that had brought us together. All the love and creativity I had was drying up and I felt like I was dying inside. I was losing my son and all that I had worked for. I became filled with rage and anger. As I got angrier, I got jealous and hateful. The real things that I wanted kept getting farther and farther away from me. I kept leaving my family. I went off searching for that "something" that I felt was lacking in my life.

My partner was working harder and harder, to the point of exhaustion. Every time I went out looking for that missing element, I lost more of what I really needed and actually had with me all the time.

Now I know that my spirit was missing, but at the time I didn't. I became lonelier and angrier. Eventually, out of self-protection, my mate shut me out entirely. I had lost my ability to love. In that place I could not do or achieve anything. I could not take care of my family or myself. I was falling.

It even got to the point that one night I went over to our house looking for a friend of hers who was visiting, wanting to kill both of them. Fortunately, no physical violence ensued that night, but terrible rage, anger and threatening did occur. I was lucky that the police arrived and got me to leave. I was in hell.

 ow does it make you feel, Michael, to be saying these things?

To tell you the truth, Angel, I hate the way it sounds, and I hate seeing it on paper. Honestly, I don't know if I want to think about these things or reveal them. I have no words. I am stunned by this remembrance.

 ichael, you said that no violence ensued that night, but terrible rage and threatening occurred. You said that you were in hell. Were you in hell as a result of that night of pounding on the door and yelling threats, or were you in hell from something before that? Had there been violence before?

Yes, Angel, there was another time. It was violent.

 hat happened?

It is so difficult to tell this. I am so ashamed and scared to reveal what happened.

 ou need to remember what you did, Michael.

One night, months before the incident I just described, something really terrible took place. I don't remember when it was — weeks, days or months before what I just told you about.

That night, in psychotic rage, I went to our home. I don't remember how I got there or exactly when I decided to go. I was in rage and passion. I was crazy with hatred and jealousy that she had been with another man. The thought of that was beyond my ability to handle. I tried to cope, but it raged inside me.

I went to her house in the middle of the night. I walked up to the porch where the front door was, and with my fist I broke a small glass pane in the French door. Then I unlocked the door and ran upstairs, my hand bleeding.

I went into her room where she was sleeping. I don't remember if she awoke from the sound of the breaking glass or if she was still asleep when I entered. My son was sleeping in the bedroom next to his mother's.

I grabbed her by her hair, dragging her out of bed, down the staircase to the living room and finally down the staircase to the basement.

At that point we struggled and fought. She bit me. We hit each other. And then I raped her.

In the morning, after spending the night there, I got up and put my clothes on and left. The basement room had blood on the ceiling and walls.

 ow do you feel about that?

I'm scared. I'm guilty. I can't believe that I could have done such a thing. I can't believe that I am capable of such horrible things. I did do it. I am a monster. I am so sorry. I am so sorry. I don't know how to atone for my sins. I should be in jail. I am in hell.

 o you think that you are the only one who has ever felt or done those things?

No, I guess others have . . . I don't know. I have no words now. In some ways I feel relieved. I feel scared and vulnerable. I should have been arrested. I should have gone to prison. I . . .

 nger, aggression and violence is the disease of the twentieth century and long before that. If people are going to reclaim their birthright as human beings, they have to understand *what has caused these terrible things to happen. I know you are sick of telling others about these things that you are so ashamed of, but if in these pages you can go through a process of healing that will bring back your love and humanity, don't you think that would be valuable? Don't you think that might be a valuable process for others in the same difficult place to know about?*

I hope so.

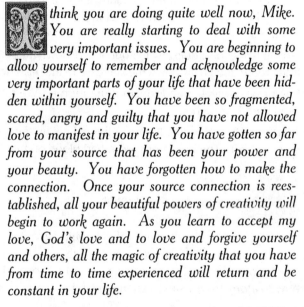 *think you are doing quite well now, Mike. You are really starting to deal with some very important issues. You are beginning to allow yourself to remember and acknowledge some very important parts of your life that have been hidden within yourself. You have been so fragmented, scared, angry and guilty that you have not allowed love to manifest in your life. You have gotten so far from your source that has been your power and your beauty. You have forgotten how to make the connection. Once your source connection is reestablished, all your beautiful powers of creativity will begin to work again. As you learn to accept my love, God's love and to love and forgive yourself and others, all the magic of creativity that you have from time to time experienced will return and be constant in your life.*

Angel, I am feeling sick right now. I have a terrible feeling in my stomach.

ou are purging a lot of stuff that has been in your system for a very long time. That in itself will make you toxic as it emerges from the recesses of your being. Also, you are delving into areas of your conscious and unconscious awareness. I know that you can't begin to figure out what that story on the Hopi reservation was really about or what it meant. At this point it is only important that you recognize that it happened, just as you must begin to recognize the connection that you and I have.

I say recognize, not understand. Please accept that there is a great deal to life as a human being that is outside the realm of logic or understanding. Please accept the premise that you cannot truly be whole until all aspects of your physical, emotional and spiritual being are aligned. You are going through that now. I know that there is much discomfort and uncertainty in this process. I do feel it is safe to say that at this point, the sickness is worse than the cure. Please continue with your healing; in the long run it will be worth it. Please continue, but remember that I am your angel, sent to you by God, and I love you. If you get only a small part of this now as it is unfolding, know one thing for sure: I love you and I love you unconditionally. I don't care what you say or what you have done in the past. Remembering and taking responsibility for that terrible night must be part of this process. You had to acknowledge it before you could get better.

A few weeks after that horrible event, a friend of mine asked me if I wanted to attend a sweat lodge at the home of Arnold Davis, a Yavapai-Apache who lives in Prescott, Arizona.

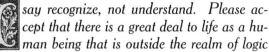

November 23, 1997

ood morning, Mike. How did you sleep?

Yesterday afternoon while I was thinking about the amazing events that occurred in the sweat lodge, I dozed off and went to sleep at my computer. Details of the experience came back to me in my dream and I can share them now.

Although I have been in sweat lodges before, this was a much different experience — very profound and mysterious.

On the day I was to participate in Arnold's lodge, I was extremely nervous about going. I knew that the more work one has to do, the more difficult the journey would be. I was very ambivalent about going into the lodge that day.

All of us who were to be part of the ceremony would arrive in the late afternoon on Saturday. We would all help to prepare the site for the prayers.

First, the ground on which the lodge structure was to be erected was cleared of any fired rocks or debris from the previous lodge. Then all of us hauled wood up the mountain a few hundred yards to the site. Adjacent to the lodge structure was a fire pit where the volcanic rocks would be heated until they got red-hot. After we brought up the wood from a truck parked next to Arnold's home, we began hauling the rocks to the site.

After the rock-hauling, the fire pit was cleaned, stacked with wood and the rocks placed in it. When the supply of wood and stones was adequate for that evening's needs, the fire was lit and a prayer was given by Arnold over the pyre that we all gathered around.

While the fire got going, we all worked to assemble the lodge. That entailed first cleaning the circular area of the lodge floor, approximately ten to twelve feet in diameter. A wooden structure about five feet high at the center, consisting of branches tied together in a half-sphere or dome, was already in place (I believe it is replaced once a year). Inside and at the center of the floor was a pit approximately four feet in diameter in which the red-hot volcanic rocks were placed. When the people, usually ten in number, crawl into the lodge, the space in the lodge is completely full. At the commencement of the ceremony all the participants crowd around the pit in the center, sitting knee to knee in a circle that utilizes all the ground space.

After the fire was started, we all worked to place various blankets and tarps over the bare wooden structure of the lodge. At completion, the dome was totally covered with the blankets and tarps. A two-by-two-foot doorway consisting of a tarp flap was constructed. It was just big enough to allow entrance into the lodge by crawling in on all fours. After the dome was finished and once the flap was closed, no outside light could be seen from inside. Likewise, no air or heat could leave the inside of the structure by way of any openings. Approximately two hours after the fire was started, the rocks were red-hot and the ceremony could begin. By that time the Sun was quickly fading and night was close at hand.

I had been very apprehensive during that afternoon and wasn't really sure I wanted to participate in the experience. I had a great deal on my mind and once again felt as though my entire world was crumbling. I was lost, confused and scared. I had lost my vision, my ability to work and to create and the dream that had brought me to this area more than a dozen years before. All the wonderful dreams I'd had in Los Angeles, which had now come true, were vanishing quickly, and I felt totally out of control and unable to correct the situation.

Just prior to the commencement of the lodge ceremony, I decided that I was not ready to go in that day. I was going to leave. Just as I was walking down the path from the lodge site, one of Arnold's dogs came up to me. It was an odd thing about this particular animal because she had always bared her teeth at me whenever I had been there in the past. In Hungarian, *farkas*, my last name, means wolf. In my entire life, I had always loved and been close to dogs. Rarely had I experienced an occasion when even the most aggressive dog did not become a friend as soon as I was in its presence. So I always thought it strange that when in my presence, this particular dog was so defensive, if not aggressive. No matter how hard I had previously tried, I could not make friends with it.

As I walked down the path, the dog, standing in the middle of the narrow trail, came up to me and nuzzled my leg. I bent down and the dog licked my face, almost to say that everything was okay and that I should participate that evening. I thought the whole thing with the dog so strange that I decided to go back and join the sweat-lodge ceremony.

As I walked back to the site, all the people were beginning to disrobe for the beginning of the lodge. This was the only sweat lodge I had ever participated in where women were in attendance. It had always been my impression that in the Indian tradition, men and women didn't go into lodge ceremonies together. Also, this lodge was attended by both Indians and Anglos. I believe the mixture consisted of Hopis, Yavapai-Apaches, Anglos and a married couple from Europe.

At dusk Arnold led a prayer over the red-hot, glowing fire pit. The heat of the pit was so intense that standing four to five feet away from it, I felt like I was getting burned. After the prayer, all of us, the men in their underwear and the women wearing bathing suits, entered the lodge. It was dark now, and one at a time on all fours, we crawled into the dark and incredibly confined structure. I found a place in the circle directly opposite the opening, maybe eight feet away. When we all finally got situated, the lodge was full. We all sat knee to knee, either with legs folded in front of us, or in yoga-meditation style. At that point the flap was still open, and once we were all inside, the red-hot rocks were brought inside and placed one by one in the center pit, which was only inches from our knees. As the rocks were brought in, the heat started to build.

At that point I started to have a terrible anxiety about being there. I was scared in a way I had never before felt. I wanted to leave. I knew that as long as the flap was still open, I had a chance to get out of there — even if it meant crawling over the upright seated bodies of four people who were between me and the opening. I tried to control my anxiety and decided to stay.

I closed my eyes and told myself this was no different from the dozen other lodges I had attended and that it would be fine in the end.

I just called Laurna at the hospital. She is so amazingly better — no fever, no infection. Her lungs are clear and she is breathing almost normally. Her lab tests indicated that her body has begun to produce blood cells and platelets and that no cancer is in her body. She is in remission! This morning she even began eating food for the first time in two weeks. All the swelling has gone also. The doctors are saying she might be able to come home for Thanksgiving in four days. What a wonderful Thanksgiving that would be!

hat is so great! I am so happy for you both. You are each in your own way beginning to heal. Please continue with the sweat-lodge ceremony.

After all the rocks were placed the pit, Arnold closed the flap behind him and began the offerings. At that moment I felt like I was going to die. I was immediately incredibly hot and claustrophobic in that small, crowded, dark sealed chamber. I felt like I couldn't breathe. Arnold began the ceremony by making offerings to the spirits, inviting them in and asking for their help. He had various herbs, sage for one, that he sprinkled over the red-hot rocks. The smoke from the burning sage burned in my lungs. All I could do was try to bend down as far as I could. I tried to place my forehead on the ground between my knees. The tips of my toes were pushed up to the edge of the tarp that covered the lodge. My legs began to cramp and fall asleep. My body was pressed up against the people who were seated on both sides of me. Although I felt like I was wedged and had no place to go, in some way there was a feeling that I was not there all by myself. I could occasionally hear the voices of the other people. Through the smoke and the light created by the red-hot rocks, I could see their dim outlines.

As I bent forward, my face on the ground only a few inches from the rocks in the center, I realized that I was in a totally prostrate position. It was the least-hot position I could find in that environment. At least for the moment, some of the Earth's coolness was still available to me, and my head was below the smoke from the sage.

I tried to control my fear. I kept telling myself that this was no different from the other times that I had done this. At those times, the entire experience was quite manageable, if not pleasurable, in terms of the purification process. But this time was different; I had so much inside that was unresolved. I was so toxic in my spirit and my body. This purification process was going to be a most difficult one.

What seemed like an eternity since I entered the lodge was in actuality only a few minutes. At some point in the next few minutes, the entire experience became overwhelming. I felt as though I was actually suffocating and would pass out from lack of air.

Arnold began to call in and make offerings to the spirits of the earth and the sky. He made offerings to the two-legged and four-legged creatures of Earth. He made offerings to the spirits of the fire and the rocks. He made offerings and asked for help to bring peace, health and love to all of God's children in all of the four directions of the Earth. He prayed for the love and salvation of the races of humankind: white, red, yellow and black. He asked that all of us in attendance in the lodge could receive the blessing of love, peace and harmony.

I was fighting to deal with the anxiety and the heat and tried to focus on what invocations were being made. I didn't know if I could last much longer. Just like that, the first round was over and the flap was opened. Arnold said anybody who wished to leave at that point could do so. I contained myself, waiting while the only other person in the lodge who wanted to leave exited.

Then I crawled out into the cold night, panting as I filled my lungs with clean, smokeless fresh air. I went over to a water hose that was nearby and drenched myself with cold water. It felt wonderful.

Within a few minutes the second round would begin. This time, and with every new round, more rocks were added to make the heat more intense than the previous round. I had a choice whether or not to go back inside. I chose to go back.

I crawled in over the people who had not left from the previous round and arrived at my earlier position. The flap was closed and it immediately became much hotter in the dome than before. I thought to myself, Why did I do this? It was too late now. Once the flap is closed, it constitutes a commitment to stay and participate.

Arnold continued to make his prayers, asking the individuals in the lodge to make their own requests of the guides and spirits called into the gathering. Alternately, Arnold would take a bowl of water and pour it onto the pile of red-hot rocks. A steam of intense heat would result. My face and upper torso felt as though they were being scalded. Once again I felt the panic of anxiety. I could no longer stand the heat and the smoke and tried to leave. I panicked — I didn't want to die of suffocation. I tried to bolt out of my position over the bodies of the people between myself and the flap. But they would not let me go! Hands reaching from around me held me in place. Loving and comforting words in several languages spoke to me in an attempt to help me control my fear. They would not let me out of the chamber. I put up a half-hearted struggle and was restrained.

At that moment Arnold began to discuss how in the presence of Tunkasula, Waken-Tanka and God, to act out of fear and to feel sorry for oneself was entirely disrespectful to the Creator. He talked about how the site where the lodge was situated had once been in the midst of a village of the Yavapai-Apache people at the beginning of the century. Arnold told of how the surrounding hills had been inhabited by hundreds of his people. He talked about how the white army came and killed every man, woman and child in the village except for his great-great-grandfather, who managed to survive his wounds. He asked of the spirits that he had called to be present for this communion to help us all be brave and to honor the dead of long ago and honor our Creator with courage.

At that moment, I became ashamed that I had been so weak and scared. I knew that I had much work of purification to do and that I was ready to stay and attempt it.

Arnold again made offerings to the spirits of the earth and sky, to the two-legged and four-legged creatures, to the spirits of fire and rock. He asked help in bringing peace, health and love to all

God's children in the four directions, praying for the love and salvation of all the races. He asked that all of us present receive the blessing of love, peace and harmony.

At that time a very strange and powerful thing began to happen to me. I had finally run out of endurance. I was having trouble breathing once again and felt as though I would expire. I could not leave, but I was burning from the heat. Then it happened. Prostrate and with total submission, I said: "Oh please, God, help me. I have no answers."

All of a sudden Arnold's words and songs, accompanied by his drum, began to fade into the background. A beautiful peace began to overtake me. The intense heat was still ever present, but manageable. A voice began to speak out of my mouth. I began to sit up from my prostrate position. Soon I could only vaguely hear Arnold's words in the background. The voice that was speaking through my voice became loud and clear. It said: "Michael, I will make this place cool for you, but you must listen."

Immediately the intense heat of the lodge became cool as the voice said it would. I was no longer suffocating and I could breathe easily. The smoke from the fire no longer bothered my eyes or lungs.

"You must learn to take care of your mate and your child. But first you have to learn to take care of yourself. Before you learn to do that, you will be of no value or help to them or anyone else. Listen to the ceremony and purify yourself and your spirit. Listen to your guides and to your God."

Soon after that the voice left and the flap of the sweat lodge was opened. We could leave if we wanted to, but all of us stayed while the next round of rocks were put into the pit. During the third round, we prayed for harmony and love in all our communities, in our nation and on Earth. In the fourth round there was a call for us to connect with the universal beings and spirits, which would allow harmony to prevail in all of God's creation.

In that fourth round, I once again left the physical connection I had with the group and began a journey of some kind. It felt as though I was dreaming. I don't really remember what happened in that dream.

would like you to go away from your computer for an hour or two and meditate on what that dream was about. I can tell you that it is very significant in your healing process. See if you can take yourself back to the lodge and into that dream place. Remember when you asked God for help? When you had no answers and felt all alone and suffocating? Mike, go to that place of total vulnerability, of ego loss and prostration to your Maker and ask for help, as you did then.

November 23, 1997, 8:03 P.M.

Angel, are you there?

 f course I am, Mike, especially now. What did you come up with? Do you remember?

I remember a dream and a trip, Angel.

 o on.

I remember when the fourth round of the sweat lodge was beginning to start. New rocks had been brought in from outside and the flap of the lodge had just been closed. Arnold began a chant and he was beating out a rhythm on his drum. Just then a voice started to speak through me, but it was different from the earlier voice. It was a woman's voice, and she was calling to me.

I remember waking up in the most beautiful place. It was like a garden, but it was so different than anyplace I had ever been to or have ever imagined. There were varieties of flowers I had never seen before. They had scents and fragrances that were wonderful, which were also totally new to me. All the colors in this place were somehow different, too. I can't really describe them. I have no words for such an experience or such a place. I remember the sky had more than one sun. Also — and this was very odd and fantastic — though the suns were out, one could still see stars in the heavens. There were stars in great multitudes.

I was lying down on a bed of some sort, and I remember waking up and being kissed by the most beautiful angel that one could ever imagine. She had pale alabaster skin, high cheek bones and big blue eyes. She had a huge amount of strawberry blond hair that fell down her back in ringlets. She was wearing a floor-length satin dress and was very tall. When she was standing, she looked seven feet tall.

Initially, I was lying down, and when I woke up she was kneeling down over me and kissing my cheek. When I woke up, at first I was startled, then amazed and then in ecstasy.

It is so funny that I am remembering all this now as I write. Truthfully, when I meditated on it, only small fragments would pop up now and then.

o on.

After I realized I was in this place and with this angel, my mind was racing. Soon I just accepted all of it and began to relax. I really have no idea how much time had passed, as I had no sense of time at all. Initially, I was pretty sleepy and felt like I was dreaming, except that it was all so real. It was more real than third-dimensional reality. It felt like what fourth-dimensional reality might feel like. At some point I sat up on the bed where I had been sleeping. The angel was sitting on the floor. Like I said, she was big, but she wasn't huge, massive or overbearing in any way. She was extremely feminine and gentle. At first I felt like a little kid in her presence, but after a while I didn't notice that there was a great deal of difference in our sizes. I know that sounds vague, but that is the best way I can describe what the experience was like.

She and I were sitting on the bed together and I just kept looking into her face. I was so transfixed by her beauty that I just could not stop looking at her. The time we spent together seemed to stand still in its exquisite beauty. We said nothing to one another by voice; all the communication was by thought.

At one point she took me on a journey that explored her realm and the vastness of her experience. I can't begin to describe it except that it was timeless and dimensionless, and it felt joyous beyond anything I can relate in words.

Than she seemed to stand up, or float up, for lack of a better description. I noticed that in her wings was a sword. She told me that she was a warrior of the realm. The sword didn't appear to be material or tangible, as one might think of a metal sword.

"My sword that you are sensing, Michael, is made of a material that can be likened to that of which suns are constructed. The atoms of the sword are as dense as any material in the universe. It is matter in its most dense state. In Earth terms, the physical weight of it would be measured in thousands of tons. I have wielded it against the most aggressive forces in the universe. It has never failed me," she said.

I asked her if I could touch it, and she said that it would not be possible. She said for me to try. As I moved my hand to within a few inches of it, I could not penetrate the space around it.

She smiled and said, "Michael, my love, do you remember when you had a sword like this one?"

I said that I didn't. She continued, "You and I have fought so many times side by side over the eons. Even on Earth, your mission now, we participated in the earthly drama so many times in the past down there. Of course, in those primitive days we didn't have swords like this one."

I looked at her and shook my head in disbelief.

"On elephants over the Alps with Hannibal, the barbarian, did we ride. In the Crusades did we live, fight and die together. On both sides did we live and die. Such drama Earth had! I hope I never have to go back there again," she said.

"The world is a stage and everybody has a part," she communicated to me. She smiled and made a funny face.

Angel, I told her, "I don't remember any of that."

She said, "That time on Earth is soon to be over. Humans in the past have played out that terrible drama of destruction and hate. You and I played our parts in that evolution. Now humanity has a choice as it comes to the end of a huge cycle. Humans can choose to continue as they have done for millennia and die, or they can become joyous, loving creatures."

She looked at me, kissed me on the cheek and said, "Don't worry, someday you will remember and we will be together again. Right now you have a different part to play."

She then said there was somebody she wanted me to meet. In an instant we were in some kind of throne room, for lack of a better description. In this place there were eight other beings like her. None spoke so much as communicated to me a welcome. In fact, they said, *Welcome home!* The entire place seemed to have no substance and no actual location. In a very eerie way it was there and it wasn't. Sitting on a magnificent chair, the only piece of "furniture" in the area was my mother!

Upon seeing her I immediately began to weep tears of joy. She motioned for me to come forward to her. I didn't actually walk over to her so much as I was just there. Still sitting, she put her arms around me and held me, my cheek resting on her shoulder.

I looked up at her with tears of joy streaming down my face and I said, "Mother, I have missed you so much. I can't believe that I am here with you now. Can this be true? Is this a dream?"

She replied in my mind, "Try not to question, just know that you are here with me and that I love you so much."

"Mother, I can't believe that you are so big and strong. I can't believe that you are an angel."

Then the most wonderful thing happened to me that I could have ever imagined. From somewhere, my dog Brownie came running into the room and hopped up on my mother's lap. Brownie, my little fox terrier from my childhood, reached his head up and licked my face and barked.

I tell you, even writing this makes me cry. I dearly loved that dog. When my mother was sick and in the hospital for all those months before she died, my dog Brownie was my only friend.

Brownie wasn't only my dog but my mother's as well. I remember how she loved him. One time Brownie got lost from our home in Alhambra, California. My mother was frantic. She put up flyers all over the neighborhood and the surrounding towns. For days she had my father drive her around to look for him. She contacted every animal shelter as far as a hundred miles away. No effort seemed too unreasonable or too difficult in her search for her dog.

After about three weeks one of the dog pounds that she had contacted called her with news that they might have her dog. His collar with his license and name was not around his neck, so it was a guess. Amazingly, Brownie — if it *was* Brownie — was in San Bernardino County, seventy-five miles away from where we lived.

With that, my mother got my dad home from work and we were off to get her beloved dog. As it turned out, it *was* Brownie. I can't tell you the tears of joy she shed when she laid eyes on him in his cage. Brownie was very sick and looked like he was going to die from distemper.

My mother gathered him up in her arms and we brought him home. She did not leave that dog's side for more than ten minutes for an entire week. He was so sick, but she refused to let him die. She spoon-fed him all kinds of things because he was so weak and thin that he could barely eat. It was the most touching thing to see how she cared for him. Brownie recovered fully from his illness. He and my mother were inseparable.

Sometimes he would hang out with me. I was eight years old and didn't have many friends. Brownie was my best friend. Often he would escort me to my elementary school that was a block away from our house. Although dogs even then were supposed to be on a leash, I don't remember his ever having one. When we went to school we would walk together, cross the main boulevard using the underpass, then he would leave me at the school steps and go about his business, whatever that was.

One time Brownie and I were on the way to school when, approaching the underpass, a huge dog unattended by any human came up the stairs and nearly startled me to death. In a second, he was baring his teeth and the hair on his back stood on end.

To this day, forty-four years later, I remember how my dog Brownie went into action to protect me. I don't think the cute little, totally harmless-looking Brownie weighed more than twenty pounds, but for a few minutes he was five hundred pounds of growling, snarling viciousness. The dogs fought for a short period of time and the big dog left. I felt as though my little buddy saved my life. I loved him so much.

I remember going home after that and telling my mother about it. She said that Brownie was my friend and protector and that he would sacrifice his life in order to "do his job" of protecting the ones he loved.

A few months after that experience my mother got really ill and had to go into the hospital. To this day, I don't know what was wrong with her or the illness she had.

My dad was at his wit's end trying to take care of me, attend to his business and see my mom. Almost every night he would leave me alone to go see her an hour away at the hospital. When I got to see her on the weekends, I was not allowed into the hospital building. I had to stand outside her window and speak to her through a screen that was high up. Brownie was not allowed to visit the hospital at all.

Over the months, this process continued in much the same way. My dad would leave me at night, and I had Brownie to play with. My schooling was a mess and I couldn't read at all. I had flunked the first grade and was on the verge of flunking the second or third (I forget which).

Eventually, my mom was well enough to take a trip out of the hospital. My dad and I were so happy. I had not been near her for months and my dad missed her more than I can describe. The day we went to get her at the hospital was one of the best days of my life. When she came out of the building she had been in for months and put her arms around me, we both cried with joy. My dad was crying, too. Brownie leapt out of the car and kept jumping up and down, up and down as my mother kept petting him in the air.

That weekend we went to a place called Marietta Hot Springs Resort. It was a few miles from Palm Springs. We were all so thrilled and happy to be a family again. Mom, Dad, Brownie and me. It was so great.

On Monday morning we took her back to the sanitarium, as it was called in those days, and I had a hope that this was the beginning of her recovery and that soon she would be healthy again and home for good.

I don't think that it was more than a month after we had taken the trip to the desert when Brownie got himself in trouble with one of the neighbors down the street. I was walking home from school with him one day when a very nasty man came out of his house and started yelling at me. He said, "That damn dog of yours has crapped on my lawn for the last time. If I catch him doing it one more time, that will be the end of him!"

I don't remember my reaction, but Brownie and I got out of there as fast as we could and went home. About a week later Brownie was dying in the back yard. He had been poisoned. The poison took him in a very slow and sad way. He kept throwing up and could hardly move around. The vet said he could do nothing for him. In a few days he was dead.

I believe that was the worst few days of my life. I cried incessantly at the loss of my dog and my best friend.

When I spoke to my mom on the phone, my dad told me not to tell her that Brownie had died. He said she wouldn't be able to handle it. For a couple weeks when I spoke to her I kept telling her on the phone that Brownie was all right.

Then, without any warning, my mom became critically ill. I was only able to see her once at the hospital before she died a few days later.

 ike, I know that it is tough for you to re-member this stuff and that you haven't thought about it for decades. I know that you have never resolved your mom's death either. Please continue.

Angel, it is getting late and I'm very tired. I need to rest and sleep. It does help me to remember all of this. I feel so sad to think of all this past stuff, but it is a relief because I haven't dealt with these things in my entire life. Much of it is so strange and surreal that I have no understanding of it. I don't even have questions that relate to it. Some of it has very real meaning for me, related to all that my life is now and was as a child.

 t is time that you sort out much of the expe-riences you have just remembered. Some of it is outside your ability to grasp. Don't worry about those areas that seem so surreal, as you called them. There are issues of the heart that you must concern yourself with now. I can tell you this: As you wake up with the experiences in the realms that you have participated in, you will receive a huge input of information. One can't just half wake up. One either wakes up and gets it all or doesn't get it at all and remains asleep. You must wake up now because you have a wife who needs you and needs you soon. The unfolding process is a big one to remember — all that we are and all that we have ever been. It is so complex and happens on so many levels. You need not try to figure it out. Just know that the process of remembering who you are is under way.

or now, all you have to feel is your heart, Mike. That is all you need right now. I think you need to go to bed now with a few questions that I have for you to think about and search for in your heart.

What are they, Angel?

want you to go to sleep and ask yourself these questions: After you lost your mom and your little dog Brownie, have you ever been able to love anybody like you loved them? Have you ever really allowed yourself to be that close to anybody since your losses as a child? Has all the love in you been buried and inexpressible in your deeds and actions for all the decades since you lost your mom? Even with all the people who really love you?

I'll sleep on those questions, Angel; but I have a question for you.

hat is it? As if I didn't know . . .

The angel in my dream, or whatever that experience was, was that . . .

e? Mikey, I'll let you figure that one out. Good night, Michael. I love you.

I love you, my angel.

Monday, November 24, 1997

Hi, Angel. Good morning, are you present?

f course I am present. Just like Laurna has nurses twenty-four hours around the clock until she gets better, I am here for you in that way until you get better.

I went to sleep thinking about those questions that you had for me, and I know in my heart that all you asked me to think about is true. My heart has been enclosed and in pain for all these decades. I cried so much then as a child. I was never able to get really close to anybody ever again. When I asked for beautiful love, it was given to me over and over again, but all I could do was push it away in the most destructive manner. I feel so badly for all those I hurt.

id you think about the experience with your mom anymore?

Yes, Angel, I did, and there is more. After Brownie jumped up on Mom's lap, she continued to talk to me. I expressed shock that she was so big and strong.

She responded, "Did you think that I was so weak on Earth that I was not or could not be anything else?"

I said, "I am so stunned and happy to see you, and see you so well and strong. I just don't get it. Why did you have to suffer so when you were on Earth? Why did our whole little family have to have so much loss and pain?"

"There is one simple reason that explains all of it. It has to do with love and compassion. The reason we suffer on Earth is so we can know how others feel in that place of hurt and loss. Once we feel the pain of others, we can have compassion and love for them."

"Does that mean that life has to be nothing but pain, loss and suffering?"

She replied, "No, my boy, that is only part of it. When people understand the feelings of pain in themselves and others, they can then begin to explore the causes of it. There are so many things that cause pain and suffering on Earth: things that people do to each other, things that people do to themselves, things that just happen that seem to be unexplainable. There are so many causes of pain on Earth."

"What happens once people discover the nature and cause of their suffering?" I asked

"They learn to love and forgive. Love, forgiveness and compassion are part of the divine order. It is the stuff of which all the beauty you have experienced here is made.

"God gave humanity free will. Humans have the choice to create heaven or hell right where they live. It is part of an evolutionary process that started from the beginning of humankind on Earth. In the divinely ordered evolution of human consciousness, the plan was that humanity could eventually realize the same everlasting bliss, love and ability to create as God had when He created the universe. It all comes from the source of light and everlasting beauty.

"All humans have to do is remember who they are. They have to understand and accept all the things that they instinctively know have caused difficulty or pain in themselves or in others. Once they forgive and learn to stop hurting, no matter what they have done in the past, they as individuals and as a race of humans will begin to heal and to have all the gifts that were intended for them. Waking up is truly a most wonderful experience once we have gone through the painful part."

"Mother, can you help me understand what to do?"

"I want you to realize that you did not cause me to die. It was not your fault. It had nothing to do with anything you did or did not do. A child can think he has caused his family to break up or has caused the loss of a loved one. Michael, my love, please know that my illness on Earth was part of something much bigger than we can understand in this discussion. Just know that you must stop blaming yourself and begin to regain the capacity to love the people around you with total and unconditional love even though you know they will someday leave you.

"You have been wondering where all your inspiration and creativity went, why it would come and go. As soon as you begin to love unconditionally all other people, including yourself, all that anger, jealousy, hate and hostility that has plagued you in your life will vanish and you will receive the greatest gift imaginable."

Mother then bent her head down and kissed me on the forehead.

Then I was there alone with Angel. I said, "Well, Angel, how did I do?"

Angel looked directly into my eyes and smiled. She reached back into her wings and drew her sword. In an instant she raised her weapon and cut me in two in a single stroke, starting at my neck and down through my body. I fell in half in one moment, and in another I was whole again. Laughing, she said, "You still have work to do. Get back down there, Michael; you are not done yet. You can't come home until you have finished your mission on Earth."

That is all I remember.

THREE

Back into the World

December 10, 1996

As dawn surely comes,
so does the eclipse of night
and the flow of consciousness.
Who are these visitors?

The body trembles with expectation.
Fear sends shivers throughout the being.
The blood runs cold and muscles tense with fear,
more fear that they are not present than here.
Please let them show themselves.

Trembling and anxious,
expectant and scared to have these
voices inhabit one's being.
Who are these visitors, and from where do they come?

It is a dark place, this twilight.

The invitation is made,
the mind put into rest and a channel opened.
The shivers that ensue.
Today these visitors are of terror.
Who are you that I have invited into my mind?
Why do I fear you so?
What is the darkness that makes me tremble?

I listen so intently for the voices.
I look so intently for the pictures.
I still my being and begin to hear, feel and see.
Who is calling to me?

The cries of ancient battlefields begin to be audible.
Bodies torn limb from limb from canon fire.
Bodies rotting, decay and stench abound.
The screams of brave and dying men going about their
insanity of noble causes.

A baby barely alive whimpers small tears,
still clutching the remains that previously had been the
living body of the infant's mother.

What force of evil had caused this drama?
Why is this beauty in desecration?
The drums roll and the caissons fire
to the tune of a fearful monster.

Bodies so thickly dense that
one could literally walk hundreds of yards and
not walk on anything except pieces of

decaying flesh.
A scene from Dante's hell.

What of this drama that is so shattering?
Why the stage, its heroes and its cowards?
Touching moments of heroism,
strangers giving their lives for strangers.
Agony of unspeakable proportions.

The voices call to me and show this story.
Tears of remembrance give charge to my emotions.
The proving ground of Earth.

These are the failed spirits of our own dark
and created hell.
They still miss the reason for their mission here.
The entire reason for humans and this drama
is simply to learn love and compassion.
There is no other reason for this manifestation.

Turn the cheek.
Send love to an opponent.
This is not martyrdom.   This is not cowardice.
This is the test of life.

For all you players in this ancient game, this is the test.
For those of you who continue in this drama,
your reward is to keep playing it over and over.
Again and again will you be
responsible for the deaths of your brothers and sisters?
The deaths of your own children?

It is your choice to listen or to be lost.
It is your choice to create hell,
where heaven can be yours.
Tremble or laugh.
It is your choice.

That certainly was quite an experience for you, Mike.

It was a wonderful thing to remember. I can't believe that I could have stashed away those feelings for so many years and not have remembered any of it until now. It was a time that I so needed to reexperience. I could have lived my life so differently if I had remembered these things years ago. I would not have lost all the people I loved and who are now gone to me. It saddens me now to realize this. I feel such sorrow, joy and relief. I feel like laughing and crying all at the same time.

I know how badly you feel about that, but that time is gone, yet those people are not. When people have unconditional love, those they love are never gone. Unconditional love is not about possession. It is not about my wife or my girlfriend or my child. Possession is not about love; it is about things. Once you love unconditionally and have that feeling for all people in God's creation, with no attachments or requirements, you become whole and are forever healed.

Love is a feeling; it is about joy and giving. Once you are in a state of love, you need nothing in return. Your love comes from the unending source of nature's essence. It is the well of nature's providence that never dries up. When you are in love, you have total fulfillment; you need nothing else but only to give your love. As long as you are in a state of unconditional love, you have everything and nothing else is needed. The people you love are always with you for all eternity.

s far as asking why this and why that and why I didn't do something then, you just have to realize that all development comes when it is ready. You simply weren't ready to receive the message before. You needed to fall before you could get it. I know it seems unfair, but that is the way it is. Right now you have a wife who really needs you. You have begun your journey back to health. You have begun to regain your ability to love unconditionally. Don't expect that to come overnight. It is a process of remembering who you are and who you have been. Patience is needed to develop long-lost abilities.

ow does it feel not to be a zombie anymore? How does it feel to light up your brain after so many years when most of its lights were out? How does it feel to have your heart begin working again? Once you start to remember and connect into the cosmic mainframe, all your experience goes from black and white and two-dimensional reality to 3D holographic. Talk about a brain-and-heart boost! Talk about liberation from possession, need, loss and the dull and boring. Wow, technicolor! Congratulations, you are beginning to live again.

I want to do that more than you know. It seems so hard to just love unconditionally and forgive others and myself. It sounds like a fairy tale. Who could do that besides Christ or Buddha?

ou called your stepmother, Shary, last week; how is she?

I get the point of where you are going with this. I thought we were going to have fun and begin to get light?

realize Shary's story isn't light in the sense of lighthearted. Her story is about light in the most important way. As far as fun, I hope you are starting to have it, because you have already written in a few days something you have been working on for years. Mike, isn't it great and fun that you are writing? Doesn't it make you happy? I can feel you are starting to let go and not judge. I am so happy for you. You are getting unstuck in your emotions and your love is starting to manifest your creativity. You are losing your fear of being who you are. Finally, you are just letting go, not judging, instead feeling protected by all those in the universe who care for and love you. Congratulations.

You know, Angel, I still have a funny little feeling in my stomach when you say those things; I am beginning to believe it.

et's hear about Shary.

I believe that Shary is a remarkable embodiment of the ability to forgive and love even those who have caused incredible pain.

Yes, Angel, I did call Shary last week and I have to say, she wasn't doing all that well. She lives in a nursing home presently, where she has been for only about three months. When she moved to New York from Los Angeles with her sister last year, she was getting pretty tired. After all, she is eighty-six years old and has been through the most unbelievable physical and emotional hardships.

It really is amazing that she has made it this far. She truly has a powerful life-force spirit that still shines. Even when I spoke to her last week, I could still hear it in her voice. I do believe that she is one of the great teachers in my life.

I met Shary when I was fourteen. She and my father married a year later. Shary was always so kind to me and tried so hard to be a mom. I think she did very well at that, considering that she had lost her two little daughters to the Nazis in World War II. I could always feel that her great loss was not very far from the surface of her emotions. All the same, her heart was open enough to mother a kid who needed a mom very badly.

She told me that in 1941 she, her husband and two daughters lived in Hungary (I forget which town). One morning she left her two little daughters with her parents and told them that she would be back later that afternoon. When she came home later that day, she learned from her neighbors that the SS (Schutzstaffel) had come and taken them away. Never did she see her daughters or parents again. Within a few days both she and her husband were also taken away by the SS. Soon she was in a railroad boxcar headed for Auschwitz; her husband was sent to Bergen-Belsen.

Shary told me most of the people who got picked up by the Nazis died emotionally the moment they were taken into custody. After being arrested, they just gave up; they died inside. Within a short time the gas chambers and incinerators took care of the remains.

In Shary's case, she told me that she would allow only two possible outcomes for her fate. One, that an American B-29 would fly over the concentration camp and put her out of her misery, and that would be okay. Or two, that she would be freed and live in the United States. Those were the only two options she would accept.

For three years Shary survived the untold brutality of Auschwitz. She said that the Sun never was visible there because the smoke from the incinerators was billowing twenty-four hours a day. She said there were always thousands of bodies piled up at the camp because the incinerators couldn't keep up with the gas chambers.

From what I could determine from her stories, she lived on virtually nothing for three years. At one time she developed gangrene in one of her hands and she "willed" it to stop. She still has the scar on her left hand.

She said she once found a turnip and made it last for weeks. She would take a bite out of it every once in a while, relish it as though it was a great feast and save the rest for another feast in the future.

She told me over and over again that her ability to survive the terrible physical and emotional conditions was derived from her trust in God and her sense of humor.

This might sound bizarre, but often Shary would have me laughing hysterically at her concentration-camp jokes and humor. Shary had been a very beautiful young woman when she was taken to the camp. She had fragile and delicate features, high cheekbones, blue eyes and thick blond hair. She made jokes about seeing her reflection in pools of water after it rained. She talked about the "miserable bald-headed skeleton" in the water and hoped that nobody would see it "because it would scare them to death."

At one point after she had been there over three years, one of the SS guards she had come to know said, "Fraulein, you are going to make it out of here and I'm not."

She replied, "I am so sorry for you."

Soon after that conversation the Russians overran the camp and took possession. The first thing they did was line up all the SS guards, their dogs and any camp officials who still remained and execute them. The Russians told her she was free to leave. She weighed fifty-four pounds and had nothing material in the world except, as she described it, "a filthy rag to wear" — in the middle of winter.

According to her story, she was eventually taken in by "the German people who owned the BMW works" in Bavaria. They nursed her back to health and eventually she came to the United States.

In my life, Shary's story is one of the most inspiring examples of the beauty of the human spirit, love and forgiveness and personal empowerment.

When I would bring people over to her home when she lived in Los Angeles, they would cry in her presence because of her great light that shone from within. Obviously, human dignity has nothing to do with the body so much as with the spirit.

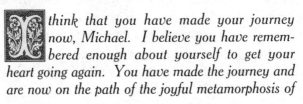 *think that you have made your journey now, Michael. I believe you have remembered enough about yourself to get your heart going again. You have made the journey and are now on the path of the joyful metamorphosis of*

unconditional love. See what can come out of that? Already you have written a book! Your creativity is coming back as your heart is opening.

I just spoke to Laurna. She is coming home from the hospital and will spend Thanksgiving in Phoenix at her brother's house. It is truly a miracle that in two weeks' time she has come back from near death. We are all so happy; I have no words for how we all feel. It's a miracle!

She will need to recover for six weeks before she goes back for her bone-marrow transplant. All of us are so hopeful. She is such a wonderful and inspiring woman, and I love her very much. I know that she is going to get completely well.

Good night, Angel. Thank you so much. I love you.

ood night, Mike. Take good care of your wife, who loves and needs you. I'll be here whenever you need me. I love you. I am your angel.

November 13, 1997

It was a dark and cold night.
No stars were in the sky.
No moon shed its light to Earth.
I went to sleep in a restless and agitated condition.
I was afraid to close my eyes for fear
of what might be seen.
As I tossed and trembled, cold shivers took over my body
as I entered panic sleep.

First, strange visions and specters invaded my awareness.
Monsters of the deep swam around me,
biting at my naked limbs.

Pieces of bloodied flesh lay in contrast
to the dark black-blue freezing waters.

More and more predators came to feast
on my still-living flesh.
Agony and fear gave way to acceptance.
A stillness pervaded the scene that had been
so frenzied, sanguinary.
A joy emerged in death. I began to feel ecstasy
where there had been terror.

By feeding the denizens with my flesh,
a completion and beauty emerged
Natural consumption was in nature's plan
that I would be freed at last
by being food to the predators. Balance was achieved
and my body no more.

A light appeared from above. First it was faint and then
it grew in brilliance.
As it drew near, it outlined the presence of angelic beings
of magnificent beauty.
What moments before had been freezing cold and darkness
became warm and luminescent.
The beings enveloped my spirit and lifted me up, up
and through the darkened void.

At once we were in an ether of breath and tranquillity.
As we ascended, stars of great magnitude and number
began to appear.
At once angels of pure white rainbows

came to greet and love.
Their loving presence raised my soul to levels of awareness
that I would have thought to be impossible and
of passionate bliss unbounded.
Such joy and rapture: music of the heaven, cosmic crackling
of stars' radiation
and signaling of a universal galactic chorus.

All at once my body returned from spirit to form.
In my veins,
transparent as a clear blue brook
in some majestic cosmic garden,
were stars. In the fluid that supported my system,
stars of tremendous
number and brightness were the blood of my body.
With outstretched limbs I could feel the energy
emanating from my fingers
as it went forth into the cosmos and exchanged
with the other lightbeings
in our celestial party.

In the stillness there were galaxies being born and evolving.
The sound of
beings at joy and creation. All shared amongst
us, travelers of the eons.

I awoke from my dream and found myself
comfortably different
in my home on Earth. All was different from before.
Our home was safe and secure,
fragrant with the smell of flowers.

My wife was happily riding her beloved horse
in the adjacent field,
the field covered in wildflowers.
She was radiant and fully returned to health,
as I have never seen her before.
My son was being dropped off by his mother
that morning so that we could
spend the day hiking together.
His mom waved hello to me
as she drove off to spend the day at the river.
My life was in bliss, creation and harmony.

The end . . . the beginning.

Dear reader and fellow traveler,

Thank you so much for taking the time and effort to read and digest the material in this book. I would find it extremely helpful and honored to receive your comments about this work regardless how you feel about it.

Michael Farkas
Fire Circle Productions
P.O. Box 1147
Sedona, AZ 86339

THE EXPLORER RACE SERIES

① the EXPLORER RACE

This book presents humanity in a new light, as the explorers and problem-solvers of the universe, admired by the other galactic beings for their courage and creativity. Some topics are: **The Genetic Experiment on Earth; The ET in You: Physical Body, Emotion, Thought and Spirit; The Joy, the Glory and the Challenge of Sex; ET Perspectives; The Order: Its Origin and Resolution; Coming of Age in the Fourth Dimension and much more!**

574p $25.00

② ETs and the EXPLORER RACE

In this book Robert channels Joopah, a Zeta Reticulan now in the ninth dimension, who continues the story of the great experiment — the Explorer Race — from the perspective of his race. The Zetas would have been humanity's future selves had not humanity re-created the past and changed the future.

237p $14.95

③ Origins and the Next 50 Years

Some chapters are: **THE ORIGINS OF EARTH RACES:** Our Creator and Its Creation, The White Race and the Andromedan Linear Mind, The Asian Race, The African Race, The Fairy Race and the Native Peoples of the North, The Australian Aborigines, The Origin of Souls. **THE NEXT 50 YEARS:** The New Corporate Model, The Practice of Feeling, Benevolent Magic, Future Politics, A Visit to the Creator of All Creators. **ORIGINS OF THE CREATOR:** Creating with Core Resonances; Jesus, the Master Teacher; Recent Events in Explorer Race History; On Zoosh, Creator and the Explorer Race.   339p $14.95

THE EXPLORER RACE SERIES

❻ EXPLORER RACE: EXPLORER RACE and BEYOND

In our continuing exploration of how creation works, we talk to Creator of Pure Feelings and Thoughts, the Liquid Domain, the Double-Diamond Portal, and the other 93% of the Explorer Race. We revisit the Friends of the Creator to discuss their origin and how they see the beyond; we finally reach the root seeds of the Explorer Race (us!) and find we are from a different source than our Creator and have a different goal; and we end up talking to All That Is! 360p $14.95

EXPLORER RACE AND BEYOND

Explorer Race Roots, Friends, and All That Is with Zoosh through Robert Shapiro

---

AVAILABLE MID-1998 . . .

❼ EXPLORER RACE and ISIS

Isis sets the record straight on her interaction with humans — what she set out to do and what actually happened. $14.95

COMING SOON

Ⓐ EXPLORER RACE: Material Mastery Series

Secret shamanic techniques to heal particular energy points on Earth, which then feeds healing energy back to humans. $14.95

Table of Contents

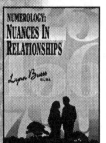

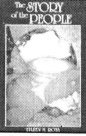

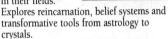

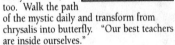